FACE

OFF

THE STORY BEHIND THE MASK

Dr. Patricia Frye
And
Contributing Authors
FAITHIN IT FORWARD PROJECT

Scriptures marked KJV are taken from the KING JAMES VERSION (KJV): KING JAMES VERSION, public domain

Scriptures marked NIV are taken from the NEW INTERNATIONAL VERSION (NIV): NEW INTERNATIONAL VERSION, public domain

Scriptures marked AMP are taken from the NEW AMPLIFIED VERSION (AMP): AMPLIFIED VERSION, public domain

Komfort Beyond LLC
P.O. Box 2681
Harvey, La. 70059
FaithinItForward.com
Dr. Patricia Frye and Contributing Authors

ISBN: 978-0-578-29508-4

Dedication

This book is dedicated to everyone who feels betrayed and confused by the struggles of life. With the hope that after reading every story you will be encouraged to move forward in FAITH.

Faithin It Forward

Everyone has a story, a background, with unexpected trials and situations in their lives. While everyone's experiences are different, our stories may be relatable and beneficial to others in ways that we may never know or understand. These experiences may include devastating losses or traumas, rejection, and many other mental or emotional challenges we have faced. Many times, we find ourselves wondering if anyone sees and understands what it feels like, who can relate to me, or have I been abandoned by God? Did I do something wrong? How can I recover?

We've seen in the Bible stories about people like Job, Abraham, Joseph, Rahab, Paul the Apostle and even Jesus and their ability to rise above hardship, their past, the unexpected losses and pain. However, you read about them but can't see them. While their stories do continue to inspire, edify, and teach; sometimes you need to see something in front of you. Sometimes you need to hear the chapters of someone's life that lives in the present. Chapters of their life that are hidden, well dressed, or seemingly invisible because they don't look like their story.

Life is full of relatable experiences that include triumphant victories! You've been wondering, where are the modern-day Heroes of Faith? You haven't been able to identify them because they don't look like what they've been through. When you read through the chapters of the lives of these authors, you just might realize you're someone's hero too!

Our prayer is that you find encouragement, strength, and restoration through these pages; and that the faith in them ignites the faith in you!

Chapter Catalogue

Faithful While Being Confronted
Dr. Patricia Frye

Have you ever felt like your entire life attracts resistance, attracts warfare? Have you ever had your pure passion for the things of God and your love for His people be misinterpreted as selfish ambition and selfish desire? What do you do when you set a standard of excellence when operating in the house of God, yet people say you're controlling and manipulative? What do you do when people, even leaders, who say they love you, betray you and work together to blackball you and spread lies about you? How do you stand when you know they are lying to and about you, but God will not allow you to open your mouth to defend your truth? If you've ever asked yourself any of the questions and need answers, I understand what you are going through. I have been there and still face it every day. I can say that, like Jesus, you have to stand and remain faithful!

I wish that I could say that being in ministry and that walking in the callings and giftings of God came without warfare every step of the way. I wish that I could tell you that the people you are called to lead will want the will of God for their lives as much as you do, as their shepherd. I even wish that I could tell you that your co-laborers in the gospel who should understand your walk and be working the harvest alongside you would be there to support you. I wish that I could tell you all of those things but that is not my truth, that is not my story.

My story includes the harsh reality that the anointing of God in your life attracts attacks. Not only do those attacks come from those who identify as enemies, but also those who walk beside you, work with you, claim they love you, and identify themselves as friends. There are people who have never and will never understand the trials that come to challenge the anointing that has been placed on your life and they are jealous of you. People will try to destroy you for something that you didn't even choose! I didn't ask for this, I was born with this. I didn't choose me, God chose me!

When I got saved, my "Yes" to God was for real. I gave God and I continue to give God my everything. When I accepted the call to ministry, I went into it with that same passion. This passion and posture have caused many lives to be changed. God has allowed me to be the vessel used to bring healing, deliverance, and breakthroughs to people across the globe. I've been called to hospitals when people were on their deathbed and, through the power of the Holy Spirit, they were made whole, and doctors were amazed. I have prayed for women with barren wombs who now have children. People who had been vexed with demonic spirits came to me in deliverance service and through the power of God have been delivered. Yet some of these same people would later come up against me to destroy me. Even going as far as telling others that I was a witch! I could not believe that they would dare call the anointing on my life witchcraft. (I mean, really, could I be a witch casting out a witch?)

Unfortunately, the warfare did not stop there. I have had a Pastor stand up publicly before his congregation and admit that he had worked witchcraft on me and tried everything that he could to kill me but none of it worked. I have had those who were supposed to be serving me while I ministered attempt to poison my drink. There have been people sent to my ministry to curse me, they have thrown graveyard dirt in front of the door, even taken photos of me to evil workers. Religious leaders who once worked with me were now questioning and blackballing me because of the lies and rumors spread by others, some of whom I once pastored. Those that once told me they loved me and were grateful for the anointing on my life were now trying to destroy me and the ministry that was charged to my hands. Yet, through it all I stood. I remained faithful.

While I kept standing and doing the work of the kingdom, while I was still praying, preaching, prophesying, and laying hands, while I was still smiling; I was portraying a strength that I did not feel. The truth is that I was hurt to the core, and no one saw my bleeding heart. I was smiling on the outside, but I was crying on the inside. All the people I had been there for and ministered to when they were at their lowest, none of them were there for me.

In my pain and hurt, I knew that I still had work to do. I was too afraid of disappointing God and of the blood that would be required at my hands of the souls that remained. Even though it seemed as if the ministry God had established was falling apart, I remained faithful. Through it all, I held fast to Matthew 6:33 – But seek ye first the kingdom of God, and his righteousness; and all these things shall be added unto you. Preaching and serving became my strength. Doing the will of the Father became my hiding place. People were passing to see if the ministry doors were closed but found the handful that remained working. I worked harder in ministry than ever before, and with less. God has blessed me and kept His promise to me that my latter days would be my best days.

While I can tell you that ministry comes at a cost and that cost can be painful, I can also tell you that it is absolutely worth it. The favor of God and His covering are worth more than any attack or warfare that you could ever face. Remember that you will never have to face it alone because

God is always there. The woman that you see standing before you today in confidence and strength has not always been. I have had to fight and continue to fight every day, yet I will stand and remain faithful knowing God will always have my back. If God can bring me through all of that to where I am now, He can do it for you as well. I do not regret all that I have gone through, as I know I have gone through to help others go through. I have stood in faith, and now I am Faithin It Forward to help others.

Dr. Patricia Frye
D.Th./M.Div/MBA/MMA/B.A./BPC/BCC

Dr. Patricia Frye is a best-selling author, playwright, entrepreneur, motivational speaker, conference host, television personality, mentor, spiritual covering, coach and licensed Christian Counselor. Many have been delivered, loosed, and set free from bondages, strongholds, and generational curses across the globe because of the Apostolic and Prophetic mantle upon her life. She is Apostle and Overseer of House of Grace Harvey, facilitator of Breaking The Silence Global Network, President of Grace Global University, and CEO of Komfort Beyond LLC. Dr. Frye's Motto is "If I Can Help Someone Along The Way, Then My Living Won't Be In Vain!
For products and services, visit www.KomfortBeyond.com

Radical Obedience

Natoia Franklin

*"For I know the plans I have for you," declares the LORD,
"plans to prosper you and not to harm you, plans to give
you hope and a future." -Jeremiah 29:11 (NIV)*

I remember the day that I resigned from my job. I had been in the education field for 11 years. I spent eight years in the classroom and another 2 1/2 years as an instructional coach for the district I was working for. I knew early on that I wanted to work with children to help them become well. In college, I pursued a major in medicine but quickly pivoted when I realized I didn't enjoy science all that much. So I majored in education, received my bachelor's degree, and eventually obtained my Master's. Although I love the art of teaching, there was a strong desire for me to go beyond teaching in one classroom at a time. I had become disgruntled with the way the education system was failing our black and brown children miserably and knew that I had to be a part of change.

While gaining more credentials in the education field, I was simultaneously building my brand as a health and wellness expert for women and children. During the day, I was an instructional coach. My job was to strategically develop plans for teachers to grow and perfect their craft. By night, I was a fitness instructor, teaching classes at my own fitness studio. On the weekends, I spent my time reflecting on some of the women that I coached. I realized that these women had been dealing with things that had never been resolved from childhood. It was their childhood traumas that led them to living an unhealthy lifestyle, gaining weight, having food addictions, and having low self-esteem.

I realized that the work I was called to do first started with reaching the hearts of young ladies for them to develop into strong women who were set free from their past. With the help of others, I developed RHYTHM (Reaching Hearts of Youth Through Health and Movement). I became very ambitious about taking this program all over my community, especially in schools.

But then, I became tired. I became apathetic about my job and felt like I was torn between two loves-my career as an educator and my wellness business as a health coach for women and children. What's more is that I had just given birth to my 6-month-old boy. Could God be calling me to quit my job mid-year, and leave behind the career I worked so hard to obtain along with my salary and benefits? Nah!!! That would be crazy! Together, my husband and I have 4 children. We are a family of 6. There could be no way God could call me to do something as silly as that!

One day an opportunity came knocking at my door. I was offered a chance to pilot RHYTHM in one school. The Deputy Superintendent agreed that if the program was a success, he would expand the program district-wide. But there was just one problem. I would have to pilot the program during my working hours. I was on a mission. I went boldly to my boss and explained the situation. I explained how this program had the potential to transform so many lives. I explained that if he would allow me one day to come in early and leave late, I would spend my lunch hour piloting this program in another school and would come back to my job. He could see my passion and agreed to give it some thought and consideration.

The waiting period to hear his answer was so dreadful. I contemplated all the possibilities. What would it mean if he said no? Would that mean that I would be stuck to continue my job, but neglect the greater purpose God put in me? If he said yes, it would be the perfect scenario. My family would have the income and benefits and I could still pursue my God given passion.

Three weeks later, I received his answer through email. It was a "No!" He felt that if he allowed me to do this, others would find out and want the same courtesy. Although I understood his justification, I was still frustrated. What was I supposed to do now? If I took a leap of faith and the program didn't succeed, my family would miss out on tremendous income. The entire financial burden of our household would fall on my husband. What if we fail?

Our Heavenly Father tells us in Jeremiah 29:11 that He knows the plans He has for us. They are plans to prosper, not to harm us and thoughts of good not evil. I meditated on that verse as well as the times He came through for me. It appears when we are in great desperation of a miracle, God moves. And that is exactly what happened to me. God moved on my heart and gave me the courage to become unstuck.

So even though I couldn't see the outcome of me taking that leap and trusting God to provide for my family, I quit my job. I endured criticism from others but had the support of my husband, which is all that I needed.

Fast forward to where we are today. We both now work in the schools implementing our youth program. Not only did we go district wide in one district, but we are now planted in three other districts.

Now I see sometimes God will push you to a place where you become uncomfortable with your current circumstances. He will use that as an opportunity to push you forward into your destiny. My faith has grown immensely. My family and community have been blessed tremendously. I learned that radical blessings require radical obedience!

Natoia Franklin

Natoia started her health and fitness journey in 2011 when she was told by her primary physician that she needed to lose at least 20 pounds. She started doing Zumba® in her basement to lose weight and soon discovered that she loved the way it made her feel exhilarated, free, and fit! She thought to herself, "I could teach this!" She became a licensed instructor in October 2011 and started teaching at an elementary school in Waukegan. After watching her sister lose 165 pounds by attending my Zumba® classes, Natoia was encouraged by her husband to pursue her wellness career like never before.

Since then, overall wellness has become a passion of hers. In addition to being a personal trainer, she has received several group fitness certifications, and in 2016, became a Beachbody Master Trainer and Certified Health Coach through the Institute of Integrative Nutrition. Natoia also created Rhythm, a dance empowerment program for children. She is committed to empowering women and children to be their best spiritually, physically, and mentally. She does this by giving them access to the tools and support necessary to be transformed from the inside out. She believes that God has given us everything pertaining to life and godliness, and that it is His ultimate desire for us to live healthy, prosperous, and transformative lives. Contact Natoia at www.serenitylifefitness.com or email at owners@serenitylifefitness.com

What To Do When You're Married in Your Head?

Ta'Keeva Payne

"Have not I commanded thee? Be strong and of a good courage; be not afraid, neither be thou dismayed: for the Lord thy God is with thee whithersoever thou goest." Joshua 1:9 KJV

It felt like life kept trying to take me out. If it wasn't one thing, it was another. I was broken, confused, hurt, numb, and alone. Those are a few words that describe how I felt at that time. How could I have allowed myself to get to where I didn't know who I was or why I was living? I honestly never knew who I was. On the outside, everyone thought I had my life all figured out, but on the inside, I was hoping that someone would come and rescue me from me.

At the age of eighteen, I thought I had everything called life all figured out. I was "grown" and felt as though I knew it all. Until my situation showed me, I didn't know as much as I thought. I was this sheltered, naive, and big-hearted girl. In this evil world where the enemy is busy, I allowed life to chew me up and spit me out. Yet, who could know that I wasn't this perfect individual? I was far from perfect, and I had no clue what I was doing.

Ta'Keeva didn't know who she was or whose she was. She was living life to the best of her ability trying to find happiness in many different places and kept coming up short. No matter where I looked or who I looked for it in, I could never find this foreign emotion. I would be happy for a little while until my "high" of that person or thing goes away. Then I was left feeling the same thing over again. I had just been promoted to a manager position. Of course, that temporary happiness was on an all-time high. I thought I had made it to a place in my life where I could make lots of cash, and it was only up from there. I was determined to become the best at what I do, and I did. Working became an addiction. It kept me busy from what was going on inside of me.

As expected, the makeshift void filler was no longer working at some point. I was on my next hunt for another. This time what I was hunting caused me to become the prey. You know when you see something new and shiny, you just have to have it? No one told me that just because it looks good on the outside doesn't mean the inside is good. A person can pretend to the point that they start believing their lies. I never knew how far a person would go to impress someone, even if it means faking.

This was the beginning of what I call my situationship. This man was ten years older than me. With my natural eyes, he was a good man. His physical features were everything I thought I wanted. I began talking, flirting, and getting to know this guy. His words were music to my ears, and I hung on to every one of them. I wanted to help him to become the best version of himself. He had much potential, and I knew I could be the one to help. The more we got to know each other, one thing led to another.

At this point, sex was involved and so was my emotions. I thought this could lead to something else. Maybe marriage, kids, vacations, you know the whole fairytale. I married this man in my head. After a few months, I allowed him to meet my family. He blended right in, and everyone liked him. It seemed like the perfect fit, and finally, my high had become heavenly.

However, my eyes deceived me. Everything I thought I knew about this man went into question. I eventually realized that I was the side chick of a long-term relationship. It seemed like I couldn't leave him alone. No matter how hard I tried, my heart wouldn't allow me to turn my back on him even though the betrayal. I desperately wanted out. I always said I would never be a side piece. Yet I became that in a matter of weeks. I'm not a homewrecker, but I became that. Like how? How did this happen?

He was feeding me lies that they weren't exclusive anymore. He would tell me all the girl's faults and how she hurt him deeply. The lies about him only being there for the kids made me feel sorry for him. I kept telling him to leave and we could make sure the kids were good. I would say to him, to fix his relationship and leave me alone. My mind and heart were at war. My mind was telling me to withdraw from this man. My heart said I love him and allow him time to get out of that situation. My cut-off game was strong one minute, but I fell into his trap when he came with his ways.

This devastation caused me to run to God. I'm a very private person who doesn't like people in my business. At that moment, I felt like I had no real wise counsel that I trusted. I needed someone who wouldn't judge me. Someone I could be vulnerable with and wouldn't tell my business to other people. I started to get to know this God person for myself. God began to comfort my shattered heart and stabilized my doublemindedness.

Since I was going to church every Thursday and Sunday, you would think that I would've left that relationship exactly where it was. I didn't realize that I had an enemy who wanted me to stay stuck in my sinful nature. He would whisper things to me as he did to Eve in the Garden of Eden. Something like, "If you love him, you should fight for it," "How can you leave that man knowing he needs you," and "Text him, call him you know you want to."

I found myself battling much in my mind. I was unstable, confused, and lost after being in God's presence. How could I have become saved but still battling with my flesh? Why couldn't I just let this man walk away forever and not allow him to come back? I condemned myself for being that girl I said I would never be. I was holding on to "what ifs." Until one day, I got tired of looking naive to this man. He saw that I kept letting him go and then come back.

I got on my knees plenty of times and pleaded to God to help me get over this man. With a lot of prayer and fasting, I was able to identify the soul ties I had with this man. God would indeed allow a person to hurt you to the point that you have no choice but to let go. It wasn't easy, but it was much easier with God. I finally used the strength God gave me to walk away from this toxic situationship.

I feel that we women start to find love and wholeness in a man without realizing it. When we emotionally invest in a man, we build our whole world around him. We marry them in our heads. Take it from someone who has been in a relationship with males since I was nine years old. I put my all in those relationships but neglected the one with God and myself. Don't be like me and waste the years of preparation because you're trying to change a man. Focus on yourself, queen. Get your credit right, go back to school, start the business, get the house, and better your relationship with God! When I prioritized the relationship between God and myself, my life became better. If He can do it for me, He can do it for you!

The Heavenly Awakening
Is Salvation

Evangelist Thais Bazile Wilson

*"He That hath an ear let him hear what the spirit saith
unto the churches." Revelation 2:29*

My journey of faith all started with a dream. I was awakened from the dream hearing the Holy Spirit calling my name "**Thais**" saying its meaning is "**The Heavenly Awakening Is Salvation.**" Now is the time for you to awaken out of sleep and walk by faith into this new journey of life I have planned for you. It's time to trust and believe by faith, I am taking you higher."

Can you imagine the fear that gripped my heart and mind? I was serving God, thinking I was doing the right thing, but doing the wrong thing all the time. I knew what God required but I was passive when it came to me. I knew there was a calling on my life and was walking in some of the things of God, but not all the way in. I was preaching one thing and living another. The Bible calls it hypocritical. I needed to be delivered. I needed to be set free. This shook me. Scared me enough to open my eyes. There were times before, God would speak, and I would be unsure about the revelation, but this time was an awakening. I heard God and responded.

Hearing this, I begin to write down by faith what I saw in the dream and what I heard the Holy Spirit saying to me. After the Holy Spirit revealed the revelation of my name, He took me back into the dream. I remember walking toward a boat. Once I reached the boat, I began to walk up stairs. I begin to hear the Holy Spirit saying, "I'm taking you on a spiritual journey in the sea of life. You cannot get anywhere traveling the route you're taking. By faith as you go up these stairs, you're taking a transition and change will take place in your life. Each step of faith you take will bring you to new levels and dimensions. Higher and higher you'll go in the spirit by faith."

I came out of the dream knowing it was high time for me to awake out of this sleep of going nowhere. For I realized salvation was nearer than when I first believed. (Romans 13:11) It was time for me to awake from a spiritual sleep of darkness and move forward into light.

At that time, I was thinking I'm too old for God to use me. However, He quickly reminded me of Abraham and Sarah who gave birth in their old age. What He did back then, He's still doing today. He is the same God yesterday, today, and forever. He changes not.

I had to keep telling myself, it's time to walk by faith and not my age. My age could not be the thing I allow to discourage me. God didn't want me stuck where I was, because of darkness and how much time I felt I had wasted. He didn't want me looking back. It was time to press forward. Time to leave the fear of what was ahead for me. He had to remind me of Lot's wife who looked back and became a pillar of salt and died. This was not His plan for me; He wanted me to live. There was nothing behind me that I needed. His plan was to do something new within me. New wine can't be poured into old wine skins. This new wine required a faith walk. This is how the Holy Spirit called me into an awakening that was a higher consciousness to walk and live by faith and trust God like never before.

I can remember the words, "Come up higher Thais, I want to use you for my glory. I want you to speak to and pray for nations. Tell them The Heavenly Awakening Is Salvation. Tell the young and the old, it is not time to sleep or be in the dark. It's time to know if you're traveling the wrong road and change direction. Now is the time to wake up, trust and see what God promised," said the spirit of the Lord. God was asking me to trust Him by faith. He assured me that having a mindset of doubt and unbelief will not get me to the promise. This time was critical for me. I had to wake up. It was time for me to take a new route in life, to get on board and travel by the boat now.

Jesus knew storms would come and that by faith I would overcome them all. Knowing He would be there through every storm, I would be an overcomer. Each storm would take me higher, making my faith stronger.

I was on a road of destruction. Praising God in fellowship and living like the world outside of fellowship. I was doing things His children are set free from. Truth was, I needed to be delivered from living a sinful unconscious lifestyle. He wanted the true hope inside of me to awaken. Looking the part wasn't going to do it anymore. (Col.1:27) This was the motivation that set me free and caused my eyes to open and my mind to be made up.

As people of God, we need to understand the hope that is inside of us. A hope that's eternal. The Heavenly awakening is salvation! This truth made me accountable for the revelation of truth that the Holy Spirit revealed unto me that day. You too will be also accountable for the truth revealed unto you. The journey we all travel here on earth should be a journey of faith.

This conviction made me say "Enough is enough." I had to make a choice. I chose not to travel this journey any longer in doubt and unbelief. I had to make a conscious decision not to live as the world leading to destruction but live the life God has created for me through the plan of salvation. It was time to repent and put on Godly characteristics that reflected my Heavenly Father. As children of God, we are called to holiness, compassion, kindness, humility, meekness, and patience. We have been called to a heavenly awakening, rooted in holiness, walking by faith in the name of our Lord Jesus Christ.

Every new day is evidence that time is getting shorter. Now is the time to walk by faith. Now is the time to repent and live the life that God has planned for us.

Stranded at the end of the road, no hope, no way out and no faith to get anywhere but stuck. These dangerous roads contain signs of doubt, discouragement, despair, and defeat. These roads leave you wounded and bruised. They are full of sin and sorrow, sickness, and discouragement. The barriers of fear, frustration and failure will rob you of joy, hope and peace; wondering if you're going to make it.

The good news is that there is a narrow road that leads to Heaven's precious promises, which is the Heavenly Awakening is salvation. There is a boat waiting to take you to the other side by faith. There are stairs to climb that will take you higher to new levels of faith. This is not a popular journey, there will only be a few that get on board by faith.

I pray that your ears and eyes are attentive to see what the Father wants to reveal to you in this season of your life. I pray your steps are ordered by the Lord and you shift to the path He would have you to take. Remember every day that you wake up is a new day and that the Heavenly Awakening is and always will be salvation unto eternity.

Evangelist Thais Wilson

Prophet Thais Bazile Wilson was born in New Orleans, La. She was raised in Marrero, La. She is the founder of Vision of Love Outreach and a licensed evangelist. Community service has always and continues to be the forefront of her life. Prophet Wilson loves spending time before the Father in prayer. She is truly a woman of faith. She knows and believes she's come this far by faith.

Through the Faith of it All!
LaTia Russell

If you read my life's story in black and white and compared it to what you see in front of you, there would be so many questions. The prefix, I'm sure, would be "how?!" How did this little black girl from a broken home, with a mother who was in and out of her life, and the prison system? How did this little black girl whose body was violated by people she knew but her voice was silenced because victim-blaming is a real thing? How did this little black girl who lost her father at the tender age of 16, whose presence wasn't always consistent in her life? How did this little black girl, who on multiple occasions considered the alternative of easing her pain by no longer existing in her earthly body? HOW?!

The answer is simple, FAITH! As a little girl growing through this world, I had no idea what my life would become, or where I would be. What I knew, is that in spite of everything that I'd gone through, somehow, I was always able to find joy. I've always known that I possessed an unexplainable amount of personal strength. I knew that even when I felt my lowest, bruised, battered & considering the worst; I was never broken. My spirit was never broken. Looking back, a word that is bolded in my mind is "perseverance." The Merriam-Webster dictionary defines perseverance as "continued effort to do or achieve something despite difficulties, failure, or opposition: the action or condition or an instance of persevering: STEADFASTNESS." They further provide "the essential meaning of perseverance: the quality that allows someone to continue trying to do something even though it is difficult" (merriam-webster.com).

For me, faith + perseverance = the woman I am today. There was never a doubt in my mind that my life would impact others in a powerful & meaningful way. From as early as I can remember, I knew that I would be successful. My father told me once that I was given four names because he thought that my name would look good in lights. So, I always made sure that 2 of my primary ingredients were always in stock. I use a little bit of each, or both depending on the situation and need. I also know because I'm built to endure, not much in life ever comes easy. As I achieve each new milestone, I reflect on the journey and several powerful scriptures that resonate with me deeply.

God's Reward for Perseverance

2 Chronicle 15:7: But you, take courage! Do not let your hands be weak, for your work shall be rewarded.

1 Timothy 6:12: Fight the good fight of the faith. Take hold of the eternal life to which you were called and about which you made the good confession in the presence of many witnesses.

2 Timothy 2:12: If we endure, we will also reign with him; if we deny him, he will also deny us.

Hebrews 10:36: For you have need of endurance, so that when you have done the will of God you may receive what is promised.

All that I have, and all that I am is because God saw fit for it to be so. It's so easy for me to explain because, without my faith and my uncanny ability to persevere, I wouldn't be here. I would not be a 2x college graduate who is working on a doctorate degree. I would not be an accomplished licensed clinical social worker positively impacting the lives of many. I certainly would not be a wife, mother, an entrepreneur, a multi-bestselling author, or a daughter with a restored relationship with her mother. I've achieved all these things because I never lost my faith when I endured all those other things. My prayers are simple and direct. I don't like to beat around the bush, not even with God. He knows I'm okay with taking the road less traveled and facing whatever obstacles may come my way along the journey. I know that at some point after I reach my destination, my rewards will come.

So many of us are walking testimonies but are afraid to talk about our journey. My sincere hope is that the person reading this right now knows, that there is plenty of faith & perseverance to go around, you just have to pull yours out of the reserve. Know that even in total darkness, you are the light. The light is within you even when you can't see it for yourself. As cliché as it sounds, our thoughts truly become our actions. And you can accomplish anything if you put your mind to it and put in the work.

There will be plenty of times where you just feel like giving up, I've been there. Where you are unable to see the forest because of the trees. The blessing in this is, once you've finally completed your journey, and you turn around, the beauty of God's creation is astounding. What I've realized through many of my life's journeys is that even when you don't think people are watching, they are. There have been times when I feel like I've gotten it completely wrong, and someone has shared how much I've helped them along their journey. Faith allows you to fully embrace that there is a lesson in everything that you do. In our successes, and well as our failures.

My faith has allowed me to be comfortable with the uncomfortable. My goal is growth and striving to be a better person today than I was yesterday. Through the faith of it all, I can confidently say that I'm okay with being a beautiful mess. It's because I know that, when necessary, my mess becomes a masterpiece, but I don't need to always have it together. Find joy in the journey. Also know that resilience looks good on you and contributes to the use of our faith as we intentionally and sometimes unintentionally shape the world. Lastly, know that choosing yourself in moments of uncertainty is always a good choice. I'm at my best when I feel centered and grounded. Being centered and grounded allows for my most important work to get done.

The "how" should be clear now. This little black girl is mixed with faith + perseverance which equals the strong black woman you see before you today. Some days a beautiful mess, most days the most beautiful masterpiece! Always a work in progress, heavily relying on the faith through it all. If I'm being completely honest, and I am, my whole life is an example of "Faithin-It-Forward," and I wouldn't have it any other way.

LaTia Russell

LaTia N. S. Russell, LCSW is a wife, mother, co-captain of a multi-generational household. A multi-best selling indie author, and co-owner of Ties That Bind Publishing, LLC.

Social Media Info:

Website: https://tiesthatbindpublishing.com/

Linktree: https://linktr.ee/TTBP20

Facebook: https://www.facebook.com/Ties-That-Bind-Publishing-107099741322396/

Instagram: https://www.instagram.com/tiesthatbindpublishing/

YouTube: https://youtube.com/channel/UConVgNgmfTzMYf1mTFhyFQw

Clubhouse: https://www.clubhouse.com/@lcswtee

But At Home
Pastor Loretta Riley

"How did I survive," was the question I asked myself for many years? The answer has always been having faith in God. Many will be shocked, surprised, and upset because no one knew about the hidden scars of what lies beneath my smile.

I was always a private person, so it was easy to hide behind the mask I wore long before the pandemic. Many saw me as an inspiration to others as I served in ministry. Doing outreach was what kept me from falling apart on days it was so hard to hold it together. I can remember so many Sundays before going to church having arguments. Many times, I cried my way there, sometimes having to stand behind the pulpit to minister. My husband would be the usher watching me from the corner of his eyes to see if I was looking at any men.

My husband was a jealous man. I couldn't even hug men in the church, because he would accuse me of having an affair. I knew what I was experiencing was abuse but wasn't clear how to address it or what kind of abuse it was. I didn't realize there were many kinds of abuse. I was not a victim of physical abuse. Being raised by my mother I definitely knew physical abuse was unacceptable. I can identify psychological abuse through the threats. Verbal abuse was mostly shouting, taunting, and creating isolation by refusing to talk for weeks at a time. However, emotional abuse is just as bad as physical abuse. It leaves hidden scars that run deep.

Due to my private nature, my family knew nothing about what was happening in our marriage because he was the best father, Papa, son-in-law, and brother-in-law my family ever had as far as they knew. All I can say is, he was a good actor.

We were married 22 years. We experienced some really good years, but in 2008 there was a change. Sickness attacked his body and it changed both our lives drastically. I became the target for what he was going through. He was very insecure of not being able to be the man he wanted to be, making me in his eyes the woman that every man wanted. After 22 years of marriage and not one time looking at any other men even after his sickness, it hurt. There were many times I cried because I was accused. I remained faithful because I was married, and I love God. In his mind it was different. Even in the tears I knew God was there for me. I am a living witness that inside of God you can survive through the attacks.

I couldn't even have a conversation with the man next door. He would peep through the door as I left the house just to see who I'm talking to. When I returned home, he would say I saw the man looking at you. I can remember so many sleepless nights because of the jealousy that was aroused in his mind. I became fond of the scripture Exodus 33:14. The Lord replied, my presence will go with you, and I will give you rest. Rest and peace are what I needed in the midst of this mental abuse and emotional roller coaster.

How do I define hidden scars? It's the scars you can't see that take the longest to heal. It's the mental and emotional wounds that leave you broken and hurting inside. I stood in faith believing that God will put my broken pieces together again. How did I survive? By the grace of God. As I revisit it, I'm glad that I don't look like what I've been through. Broken and shattered but I am still here.

Out of all the years of suffering and abuse I held onto my faith knowing that this too will pass. God will restore everything that was lost. The Bible says in 1 Peter 5:10 "and after you have suffered a while, the God of all Grace who has called you to his eternal glory in Christ will himself restore, confirm, strengthen, and establish you." This scripture is good news. God will put you back together right in front of the people that broke you. That's a Hallelujah moment for me.

Many times, I will look up and say, "God where are you?" I stood on Psalms 23:4 even when I walk through the darkest Valley, I will not be afraid for you are close behind me, your rod and your staff protect and comfort me. How did I survive? Faith in God.

As years went by, I waited for a change, and I knew when the time was right the Lord would make it happen. God's perfect timing does two things. Number one, it grows our faith as we are forced to wait and trust in Him. Number two, it makes certain that God and God alone gets the glory and praise for bringing us through. Many days I would watch the clock when it was time for him to come home and pray he was in a good mood because I didn't want to fuss. I just wanted peace of mind, to feel comfortable at home which should be my safe place.

There was never a doubt in my mind that my husband didn't love me. There was nothing too good for me, but because of his insecurities he became uncontrollable. It caused me to feel like I was sleeping with the enemy. I was determined to stay with him because I felt it was my job to be there, mainly because he was sick. All the while, the verbal abuse was getting worse. The name calling, and words you would not think a husband of 22 years would say to his wife was unbearable.

In 2019 when he told me after an argument that he will show me, I believe it was the way he said it and the look in his eyes that I knew right that moment that something had to break if I was going to survive. That moment was the exit for me to run for my life. It was like a bright shining light in the kitchen. I will never forget that day. He was at the stove cooking, and I began to prepare to leave. I was packing still in unbelief I was leaving my husband something that I never dreamed of.

I found an apartment and surprisingly he helped me move. The blessing was we remained friends. He would come over and watch the game and sometimes still try to argue, but I would tell him that's over with get your hat and go. It was then I gained my life back and was able to stand up and protect myself from verbal abuse.

After 22 years to put the key in the door, knowing you are now at a place of Peace was such a wonderful place to be. The silence in the house was now where my soul was free, no more chains.

The Lord called my husband and my friend home on December 31st, 2021.

So many women are dealing with abuse and don't know how to get out. The encouragement is don't stay in a relationship just to say you have someone. You deserve better, know your worth and protect your peace.

Pastor Loretta Riley

Loretta Riley was born and raised in the city New Orleans La. She considers her faith and family the most important to me. She started working at the age of 16 as a part time worker in retail. By the time she was 20, she was in management. In 1999 she started an in-home daycare while working part time doing private duty. Riley started working for peristyle assistant living in 2017 part time, working two jobs and being in ministry kept her very busy. She often worked because it was my escape from being home facing adversity. Her job became my place of peace. In 2019 she became a house manager over one house and in 2020 was promoted to Director of Operations, now overseeing five houses. Loretta always was a hard worker and believed that the sky is the limit to what she could have or accomplish. Loretta states, I was always labeled as a (Woman Of Faith) by where my Faith was tested much. She received many awards of dedication, faithfulness, commitment, and reliability while working in ministry. She was ordained as a pastor in 2003 and is founder of (Power, Anointing & Love outreach ministry. She enjoys spending time with family which includes 2 daughters,7 grandkids, and 4 great grandchildren. They are her motivation. Her confession is "I AM A Survivor."

Pushing Through Perseverance
Prophetess Kiesha Lynn Keller

"I will lift up mine eyes unto the hills, From whence cometh my help. My help cometh from the LORD, Which made heaven and earth." Psalms 121

As a former domestic violence victim, prostitute, and Madam, I can say the Lord has been more than good to me. I am a product of the saving grace and deliverance of God. Through my deliverance and transformation by the spirit of God, I began to understand my assignment. Through my former lifestyle and experiences God gave me a passion to start a nonprofit organization called Esther's Haven House. Through this organization we provide homes for homeless, HIV, and breast cancer patients. We also provide re-entry for those that were formerly incarcerated. I know what it was like to need a way of escape and the ability to start over through more than one experience in my life. My desire became to teach women independence and provide non-traditional forms of purchasing homes for those who couldn't qualify the traditional way.

Understanding the assignment and fulfilling it, is never said to be a walk in the park. Matter of fact it is the assignment itself that causes you to continually be tried on what seems to be every side. A roller coaster ride are the words that come to mind when I consider these past 12 years of my life. Loss after loss. His and Lows. Process, progress, and process again. Many see, but few know the things one goes through to get where they are today. Oftentimes we are just holding on by a string, and my string is God himself.

During the aftermath of Hurricane Katrina, I lost my home and everything that I owned. I became homeless and my husband was in prison. Putting the pieces back together seemed impossible, long, and hard.

Starting in 2015 was the first of 5 surgeries. I was injured on my job at the time as a traveling nurse, being attacked by my patient. I had surgeries on my shoulder, neck, back, and hip twice. There was no workman's comp, therefore I had no income. All my resources had been shut down. I was unable to get any assistance or help. At that time, God was calling me to a place of total surrender and casting all my cares upon him. The only response I had was by action, and that was to get in the press. To press into God in prayer and in scripture. I began to Incline my ear to God to see what He was requiring of me. It literally caused me to focus and realign myself spiritually as well as naturally.

The year 2016 was a time of total devastation. My brother-in-law, brother, and husband all died in the same year. I felt lost, broken, and empty, but before throwing in the towel I had to consider Psalms 23- The Lord is my shepherd. I had to hold on to that verse in my mind as I navigated again through what I considered another devastating loss.

After my husband passed, it wasn't enough to feel alone, but then I felt great disappointment from the place where I worshiped. It wasn't until I was on a walker barely getting around when I experienced total disrespect from another minister in the church because I needed to sit closer to the front. My pastor allowed the disrespect and yielded no consideration for my condition or as a co laborer in leadership. Other things began to transpire that I was not in agreement with, such as being asked to antagonize other members to leave, because they weren't liked. I witnessed clicks in leadership, absence of training and positioning those who can be manipulated and controlled. This was a hard pill to swallow because I had served at this ministry for years in labor and in seed. As I was experiencing this, at what I would consider my lowest time, I made a conscious decision along with my doctor's recommendation to remove myself from the assembly.

Initially, I had struggled with leaving the church because my mother attended there as well. At that time, I was my mother's caretaker along with my living brother. She had been diagnosed with early dementia. With my dysfunction and her sickness, I felt it was the best decision at that time. It was enough I had not yet gotten over the loss of the men in my life, surgery after surgery and being partial caretaker of my mom, but now it seemed my spiritual support system was collapsing. Again, I was pushed in the press.

The Lord continued to push me to expand my nonprofit organization. He instructed me to go to Mississippi and acquire three additional houses for the organization. Through obedience, there was no struggle. Provision had already been made by the time I arrived. We were now able to house 30 more individuals that were displaced or needed reentry. In 2020, the spirit of the Lord gave me a desire to go back to school. With all that I had going on, He redirected my attention to continue to advance myself and through nursing continue to use my gifts of help. As a result, I started school and am currently pursuing my degree.

Then in 2021 I lost another brother. In losing him I became full-time caretaker of my 80-year-old mother with dementia. Now the roles have changed. Where my mom once took care of me, I am now taking care of her. Feedings, putting her to bed, always being conscious of where she is and what she's doing; checking in on her at night, encouraging her when she feels ashamed because she can't do the things she used to do.

Even with the demands of being in school, still suffering chronic pain from my injuries and taking care of my mom, I continue to trust and depend on God for my next move. The assignment doesn't end because the load is heavy, it just keeps me persevering.

In recording these life changing events in my life, I feel it's imperative to those that read it to understand that life will bring challenges, but God is always in the midst. We have a responsibility to respond to God during challenges to understand that there is more to life than what we see. In the midst of everything going wrong, it's the things that God divinely does that we couldn't do that makes the difference. Losses come to push us into a place we once were in God or have never seen before in Him. In the press you receive instructions and strength. God will begin to awaken desires, gifts, and ambition you had no clue existed. In a place where I may have once been unsure, in this season of my life I am confident that God is up to His best work yet.

Is it hard? Yes. Some days I don't know what's going on, But I remain sure in His word that He is my help. There is not a thing in my life that I have acquired without God.

Always remember 1 John 4:4 – Ye are of God little children and are overcome because greater is He that is in you than He that is in the world. The greater one that's inside of us will continue to guide you to complete the assignment. As I keep my eyes fixed on God and allow the greater one to lead and guide me, not only will I keep to the assignment, but I look forward to all of the promises of God coming to pass that He has predestined for me. Never give up. Persevere and press and God will do just what He said. Trust the process.

A Mother's Heart
Prophet Phileshun Sylvan

Every mother from the moment they are pregnant, have concerns. They prepare to ensure their baby is healthy. Try to eat and drink the right things, take prenatal vitamins and everything that comes with ensuring we do our part. When the baby is born, there's such joy and blessing witnessing an extension of yourself strong and healthy. A mother nurtures and cares for her child to keep them healthy, safe, and loved. I did this, as any mother would.

Imagine getting a phone call and it's your brother on the other end saying something is wrong with your son. What do you mean something is wrong with my son? Something's not right, and you need to see what's going on with him. I didn't realize that this one phone call was about to change my life drastically.

The evening of the phone call, I went home after working long hours and called my son into the room. To my surprise, I could see it. It was all over his face, something was wrong. He doesn't look like himself, and certainly he didn't sound like himself. He was talking to people that were not there. Something was happening in his mind. At this time my son was 18 years old. He didn't think anything was wrong with him, so I couldn't force him to go to the doctor. I had to convince him that I was sick to get him to go to the hospital.

I remember writing down triggers to slip the doctors so they could be scripted as to what to say to get the response, which would be evidence of what I was claiming. After witnessing it, they had to call the police. Not to rough him up, but the procedure was the police had to come and get him and bring him to a facility.

I felt helpless, hopeless, embarrassed, and condemned. How did this happen? One day I have a healthy child and the next day he is mentally ill. My world was turned upside down.

You must understand my thinking at this time. I am a minister, and I believed my son was now under demonic possession. For this to happen my former sins must have caught up with me. Imagine the torment that was going through my mind, my sins falling on my next generation. I thought I was reaping what I had sown. I've committed so many sins outside of Christ and this is the consequence.

The medicine didn't work. I went months trying to get him help. I had a sense of hope as I saw others with this condition that was controlled with medication, so I did everything I possibly could to get my son to a place of stability. It wasn't until he got in trouble with the law, that I was able to get help. When he went before the judge, they called in a psychiatrist and were able to get him diagnosed and treated.

It was a relief to see the medication made him stable, but it caused emotional instability for me. Living with the constant fear of someone taking advantage, hurting him or him hurting himself. He's an adult, and I can't hold him hostage. The sleepless nights filled with worry and fear of him being safe. The torture of thinking that my sins had fallen on my seed was a constant battle. My husband sought to encourage me. He gave me a visible example within his family to remind me that it could be worse. While he viewed it as a blessing, I viewed it as God being merciful. I was just grateful that my other son did not have this sickness.

Then three years later, another phone call added additional weight to my heart. My oldest son called. I could hear it in his voice, he was different. He too was diagnosed with a mental condition. Once again, it took trouble with the law to get him help. I remember him having an episode when I received a phone call to pick him up from a homeless shelter. I drove from Louisiana to Texas to get him, and when he got in the car, he said he wanted to kill everybody. He ended up in the mental institution for months.

I thought I was cursed. I remember saying, "God, you continually bless me with physical things, houses, cars, etc. but how can I enjoy them when my sons are sick?" Seeing other kids became a constant reminder of what I will never have. The visions a mother has of her new baby won't be my reality. No college, marriage, etc… My emotions were all over the place.

From the position of a mother to a minister I was being tortured. What's going to happen to them when I transition? Who's going to take care of them? God if they are not mentally capable, how can they choose you as their Savior? Will this happen to my grandkids? Will I keep my sanity? These thoughts became a lifestyle.

I traveled and paid lots of money for my children's healing. From revivals to prayer lines, to prophets and saw no manifestation. Where is Jesus on the earth? Where is my power? I couldn't pray it away. I couldn't fast it away. I just had to live with it. At some point we did come to the realization that mental illness ran on their dad's side of the family. It skipped a few generations and ended up a part of my sons' adult life.

You think when your kids grow up that your responsibilities are minimal, not for me. We went through tons of medications. Side effects from one not being able to walk, to another mouth twisted and several other instances. Back and forth to doctors and hospitals and trying new prescriptions.

Here 8 years later, I am grateful my sons both live with me and are stable. They know the word of God and often worship with me. I watch them to make sure nothing unusual is happening. I give them their medicine daily, otherwise they won't take it.

Though at many times this has been a torturing experience, I am committed to believing God for my sons total healing. I believe God will get the glory out of my pain. I stand firmly on healing is the children's bread. This experience in my life has birthed a passion for the mentally ill. No one knows their struggles, their pain or even consider those who care for them.

As a mother the most helpless feeling in the world is to have a sick child you can't help. However, the sobering experience is having the unconditional love of my husband, my biggest supporter here by my side. His willingness, compassion, and relationship with my sons is like none other. I am forever grateful that the Lord allowed him to be my partner in this journey.

My greatest comfort is in knowing that the Lord is with us. He watches over and protects beyond my ability. The Holy Spirit quickens and strengthens me, and I know Jesus is seated on the right hand of the Father making intercession for us. My constant inspiration is knowing and believing that all things work for the good of those that love the Lord, who are called according to His purpose.

Prophet Phileshun Sylvan

Prophet Phileshun Sylvan is the founder of Jesus Christ Labourers for Souls Ministries. She is also joint owner of Sylvan Construction Inc. She is a Real Estate agent, wife, mother of three with two grandchildren.

Prophet Phileshun Sylvan works diligently in the community to help improve the quality of life for hurting people by providing food, clothing, and other essential needs.

Phileshun also works in the Real Estate industry building residential and commercial properties. Helping people become homeowners and leaving and inheritance for their children is one of the many things Phileshun is passionate about.

Phileshun lives her life by the first two commandments of God. Thou shall love the Lord thy God with all thy heart and with all thy soul and with all thy mind. And the second is like onto it Thou shall love thy neighbor as thyself.

My Faith Is A Decision, Not A Feeling

Sabrina Robertson

In a powerful sermon preached on September 06, 2020, Dr. John Maxwell admonished believers to understand that "A faith that cannot be tested, cannot be trusted". Resolved in the face of what could accurately be described as the deadliest pandemic of their collective lifetimes. With empathy and understanding he resonated with the mounting death tolls, unrelenting emergence of new variant strands and the impact of an economy and national government seemingly on the brink of collapse. Validating the truth of their physical realities and shared experience his message stood as a prompt to shift their hope from the potential outcome of their current circumstances to the everlasting security that could only be found in their unwavering faith.

Hebrews 11:1 explains that "Faith brings our hopes into reality and becomes the foundation needed to acquire the things we long for. It is ALL the evidence required to prove what is still unseen" (TPT). Faith is defined as belief, firm persuasion, assurance, firm conviction, and faithfulness. Faith is trust in what we hope for and assurance that the Lord is at work even when we cannot see it. Faith recognizes God at work in all situations at all times! It is in this sacred space of assurance, even when we cannot see it, that as believers, we find refuge and solace in times of adversity and trouble. While religious faith and faith like behavior can be influenced and taught, the life sustaining faith that anchors our souls must be lived and developed through a process of testing and time.

In 2017 I went through my own testing process that both shook and surprised me; up till then, I had lived an emotionally comfortable life. I had my share of ups and downs, but nothing too extensive and certainly nothing impactful enough to shake my faith in God. By the age of 40, I had a daughter in college, money in the bank, a respectable social circle and a professional reputation that was thriving. I had even managed to become a sought-after therapist, speaker and professional program mover and party host. So, you may be asking yourself what happened? Believe me there are days when I still ask myself that very same question. While I can't blame my plight on any one person or thing, I must say that societal pressure and my ticking time clock certainly had a role in influencing my ability to make good, sound decisions; you see despite all my accomplishments and success I was always faced with the one question that I never seemed to be able to answer: Why aren't you married? It was never asked in a rude or intrusive way, in fact most people displayed a general sense of concern and bewilderment that usually sounded something like: "OMG, I can't believe you're not married!!! But you're so funny or smart, or intelligent or pretty" as if despite all of that, I was still lacking and bottom line not good enough.

In 2016, I met, dated, and became engaged to a man who, three months later, I discovered wasn't mentally or emotionally available. That single experience in such a short period of time nearly destroyed my life. We had the wedding of my dreams in early 2017; three months later, things started to fall apart at the seams, and six months later, it was all over. He moved out. I was left with almost no money in the bank, more bills than I had before, and a mental and emotional state that was now in jeopardy. Add to that my pride and joy, and motivation for striving had dropped out of college and was expecting a child. My grandson, whose impending birth at the time threatened to be the straw that could break the camel's back, turned out to be my saving grace. He was sunshine on some of my darkest days.

For days, I sat in my bedroom in utter bewilderment teetering between feeling stuck in the Twilight Zone and wondering why God had chosen to forsake me. I cried more than I slept as I anticipated the damage being done to my reputation, feeling like I was in financial ruins and the reality that not only was the honeymoon over but so was the marriage. Despite my own personal collapse, I continued to see clients and serve in ministry. My life was falling apart, but I refused to give myself permission to NOT be okay. I shut out almost everyone, telephone calls were kept to a 5 min maximum, and I relied heavily on my therapeutic skills to compartmentalize and cope during the day, while at night I found myself taking inventory of all of the reasons I had to live another day. Understand, I was never suicidal. I never wanted to die, but I would be dishonest if I pretended that there weren't moments and whole days even where it just felt like not waking up would be easier than going outside to face another day. It was in those moments where God extended to me a phenomenon I would later come to know as, Greater Grace! It would manifest itself in various ways at different times, but it most often took the form of five very specific people who loved me enough to notice that I was in pain and refused to let me sink. Though the pain seemed to paralyze me, in reality I was surviving day by day, minute by minute, moment by moment.

My intervention came about a month later when my accountability partner said, "It's time for you to make a decision, you can become bitter, or you can become better. The choice is yours". That moment revealed to me that my healing and recovery was MY decision! I began praying and asking God to show me my role in the situation, which shifted the focus from what happened to me to what I allowed, contributed to, and inspired. Accepting that I had traded God's will for my own, opened the door for God to reveal to me every red flag, speed bump, and road flare that I had ignored, sped through, and plowed over to get what I wanted. At that point, I stopped looking at the other person and committed to recognizing every deficit and pride-induced tendency that allowed me to create loopholes to circumvent the standards I'd previously held. That kept me so busy that I didn't have time to nurture or harbor any feelings of hate or bitterness. With the backing of my support system, I went on a two-month ministry sabbatical, I took some time off from work and only saw clinically fragile clients. I went on a fast that isolated all forms of negativity in my life, including cutting off communication with anyone who was not speaking life to me about my situation. You see, the people who loved me were looking for an explanation, some wanted vengeance, and others simply wanted blood. But I couldn't let myself get caught up in that because it was truly a perish or survive situation for me at the time. So, while I didn't absolve anyone of their feelings, I did assure them that they didn't have to hate him on my behalf; I'd decided that vengeance was God's business and being blessed was mine.

Refusing to be embarrassed, I accepted the fact that no one could tell my story better than I could, and once told, it couldn't be used against me! Here I am five years later, still standing, restored, smiling, overcoming, and closer to God than I've ever been. During that time, I cried out to God from places I had no idea existed, and I came out the other side convinced of the following truths: ALL things work together for my good (Romans 8:28), and my faith does not make life easier; rather, it makes me stronger.

Sabrina J. Robertson, LCSW

Sabrina is a Licensed Clinical Social Worker with over 20 years of social service experience working with children, their families and the vulnerable adult population. As a result of being raised in the Christian Community of the Bay Area and living in the community in which she serves Sabrina has developed a rich sense of cultural competency that has allowed her to work successfully with children and families of various ages, stages and backgrounds both professionally and spiritually.

When not pursuing professional goals, Sabrina can be found worshipping and serving joyfully in the capacity of Ministry Coach at Praise Fellowship Bible Church of Richmond, California under the leadership of Senior Pastor, William Coleman, III, where she has been a member since 2009. She is the host of the popular radio show "High Tea with Bri" and she is a regular guest host on the Stellar Nominated radio show "Shop Talk" both airing weekly on FreedemRadio.com. In 2021 her first book, *The Pain of My Inheritance: My Mother's Wound* debuted on six of Amazon's Best-Selling list. To round out her many accomplishments Sabrina is a proud member of the illustrious Delta Sigma Theta Sorority, Inc.

She is the proud mother and Yaya to two beautiful grandchildren.

Simply put, Sabrina is a lover of God and people! She is known for her trademark smile and quirky sense of humor; guided by the principle of Proverbs 17:22 "A merry heart doeth good like medicine; but a broken spirit dries up the bones". Sabrina finds a way to infuse love and laughter into her professional and ministry capacities making her a sought-after therapist, speaker, program host and radio personality.

From Bankrupt To Breakthrough

Dakelah Guishard

It felt like the end for me. Leaving a 3-year failed relationship at 23 with a 2yr old baby and filing bankruptcy. Not to mention the fact that I didn't have a college degree. Instead of seeking God for guidance after the breakup, I was out living a happy (broken) single life. The year Covid 19 hit the country was when I began to save money like I never have before. This same year we moved to Texas. God knew what he was doing, but I didn't.

I don't know how to explain it, one day I just felt different. I was nauseous, and noticed I was always sleeping. So, naturally I decided to take a pregnancy test and it was positive. At this moment I was mad, angry, frustrated and upset. "I can't have another baby; I'm going to Texas single and with one child" was the only thing that was on my mind. Then the thoughts of starting over with a newborn baby. Battling in my mind and emotions, I made the decision to have an abortion and keep it to myself. I set an appointment and went in to start the process. The nurse called me to the back, did blood work and did the ultrasound. Instead of leaving with "my" desired outcome, I left with an "It's a boy". To my surprise, I was five months pregnant.

This is when I can truly say God completely stopped all my plans and started realigning His will in my life. He knew where He desired to take me and if I had that abortion, I would've continued down the wrong path. At this point, I knew I had to get myself together and used most of my savings on getting things for the baby. During this time, it was a dark moment in my life. I was very disappointed in myself. I felt like I had nothing to offer my son, let alone another child. This pregnancy was different from my first one.

I was full of fear. My relationship with God was weak and the devil knew it and played on it. From sleepless nights thinking that I wasn't going to wake up in the morning, to seeing other pregnant women catching covid and passing away, I was completely scared. He really taunted me from the time I found out I was pregnant to the day I had my son. I even went extreme and created a video for my firstborn, out of fear of not making it out of labor & delivery. The depression was heavy on me. I would sleep all day, but once everyone else was asleep the devil was back in my ear. After having my son it's like the enemy finally left me alone. Then 2 weeks later I lost my grandpa, and that added to the depression.

I stayed in my room with the baby all day. We were in and out of the doctor's office because he was always sick. He cried nonstop sunup to sundown, and one day I just had enough. I called my doctor and told her I think I have postpartum depression. Little did I know this was the day that God was turning everything around for me. I packed my son's diaper bag and drove around for an hour crying to God asking Him what I was doing wrong, and I invited Him into my life to lead me. From the failed relationship, 2 kids, filing bankruptcy, and depression it was evident I could not lead myself and had fallen completely down.

After that encounter with God, I started to only listen to gospel music, read the bible, and watch sermons every single day. Our relationship was stronger than ever, and I could tell from my perspective on things that He was shifting my mindset and atmosphere. I would talk to Him every day whether it was good or bad. I really submerged myself into His word. While doing this I knew I had to get a job to provide for my boys, so I started applying. Literally, every job that I applied for would not hire me. I was even willing to accept less pay than I deserved, but still could not get hired. This is when I went to God asking him what did He want me to do? Am I supposed to work, or was there something else for me? He gave plenty of signs on the job offers that I did get, of them not being for me. It was not until I was fasting for 21 days seeking an answer that he finally showed me what I should be doing.

I prayed many times before making the investment. If there was one thing I did know; it was that I did not want to do it my way anymore. After He showed me that this was my path, I started studying real estate investing. I also invested in myself by getting a mentor. I started my Airbnb Arbitrage business and in a little over 90 days I signed my very first agreement in my company's name. This was big to me. I did it! I listened to God and watched Him not use my past against me but built me through it. I made my first big accomplishment without a degree and bankruptcy on my name. He had completely shown out on my behalf, and I am ever so humble and grateful.

Then suddenly that dark cloud crept up on me like a thief in the night. This past December I received the worst call of my life. My cousin Kameron, who was more like my brother, was taken from us. My world crashed instantly, and I started to question God. "Really God after I have done everything you had asked of me? After I let go of all the bad habits? Why him God? You really only gave him 20 years of life? God whyyy?. All of this was going through my head, and I started to get filled with hatred and anger. I just didn't (still don't) understand why this had to happen. My entire family was and still is grieving over losing him, and it just doesn't seem fair. Through all of this, I am learning the importance of keeping God-fearing people in your circle. My friends prayed and uplifted me daily through this season of my life. This and along with my 2 boys helped me continue in my business.

Now I am currently writing a book and my business now offers credit restoration. As well as fixing my credit and getting the bankruptcy removed. I am aspiring to soon become a coach to teach others how to start an Airbnb Arbitrage business by faith and build generational wealth. My mission is to help those who filed bankruptcy become homeowners, learn financial literacy, and build generational wealth while having faith. God brought me from bankrupt to breakthrough and now everything I'm doing is only because of His grace and mercy. He qualifies the unqualified and I'm one of many examples of that. I'm a strong believer that if he did it for me, then he can do it for you. It took me changing my environment, being isolated, and being separated for Him and in Him to see my purpose. If I had received all this back in Ohio with my old mindset, I would have ruined it all. He knew the old me could not handle this big of a blessing and guess what He was right.

He's still working on me every day. There are still challenges that I face dealing with losing my cousin, however, I know God is by my side and if He's for me, who can be against me. He has proven it numerous times and I know He's not going to fail me now.

Dakelah Guishard

Dakelah Guishard is the proud mother of two and resides in Arlington, TX. She is the author of From Searching To Superhost Over 50 Super Points To Start Your Airbnb Arbitrage Business By Faith. She is also the owner of Key to Your Home Solutions LLC with the mission to help those who filed bankruptcy build generational wealth, become financially literate and homeowners by faith. Dakelah currently facilitates Airbnb Q&A Consultations and Airbnb By Faith Academy via Facebook.
Connect with Dakelah
www.keytoyourhomesolutions.com

The Unloved Child
Annette Flemings

This is a story about a little girl that was looking for love in all the wrong places. I had the desire every daughter had, to be loved by their dad. My father was always in my life, but wasn't really a part of my life. My parents split up when I was between 1 and 2 years old. I was too young to remember living under the same roof with them together. I do remember my dad would pick us up in the summer. We spent time at his house, but he was never there. We were really spending time with his new wife and my other four siblings. Even though I knew who my dad was, it was like I really didn't know him. The thing I can remember as a child being at his house is when he did get off from work, he came in, dropped his bags down on the floor, spoke and went straight in the room to talk with his wife. When he came out of the room, if he had any corrections or discipline for us, he gave it and went straight out the door.

I was numb and hurt all at the same time. I truly never had a relationship with my dad. He wasn't a good example of how a man was supposed to love me, treat me, or even compliment me. I never saw it or experienced it. My mom remarried, but again it was the same picture, a man in the home but still can't remember a father daughter relationship with him. Every time my mom took us somewhere as a family it was always my mom and her kids. Or my mom with her sisters and their kids. No man present to be an example.

The absence of what I was desiring caused me to be angry. I loved to fight. Especially boys. They could say one wrong thing and every ounce of numbness and pain would be triggered and that would be my moment of release. Aside from fighting, I always did things that I thought would make me happy like going to church, singing in the choir, running track, taking piano lessons, and doing gymnastics. I was so good at running track until I received a lot of positive attention. I was happy not because I always came in first place, but because I was finally getting attention, or should I say the love I had been looking for. At least that's what I thought love was.

I used to always see all the kids' parents out there and didn't know why my parents never came. When I got home, I asked my mom to come watch me run but she had to work. As a child I felt she didn't care or didn't love me, but as I got older, I realized that it wasn't any of those thoughts. She had to work to make sure we had the things we needed, not the things we wanted. My father on the other hand just didn't have time.

My mother started having children at a young age. She never was a person that said I love you, but I knew she loved me because of the things she did for me. I can remember like yesterday the first time my mom told me she loved me. I was 10 years old getting ready to leave to go out of state to run cross country track. I just looked at her not knowing what to say or do. Finally, I just said I love you too, because I felt that was the right thing to say. As far as my dad, let's just say he never told me he loved me, hugged me, even kissed me, or showed any type of love or attention I needed. I never felt loved by my dad. I can remember one day calling my dad asking him for eleven dollars and fifty cents, to buy some shoes and he told me no, go ask my mom. He said he already gave her some money for us. Of course, I didn't understand then what he was talking about. But now as an adult I realized he was talking about child support he was paying.

He didn't like the idea that he had to pay my mom $125.00 a month for six kids. I can clearly remember that amount because being their last child, my mom just gave me the check. My dad meant he wasn't going to give a dollar over what the court said he had to pay. It didn't matter if I had a pair of shoes to wear or not. So as a child I felt he didn't care where I was concerned. Imagine the emotions of wanting someone to love you back so bad and they refuse.

The only memories I have of me, and my dad was him taking me fishing one time. I also remember the flounder I caught. Looking back, I guess he did love me because when I got kicked out of school for fighting, he allowed me to come live with him so I can go to school from his house.

At some point, I realized my relationship with men was set up for failure. I didn't have God as the head of my life, neither knowing how to treat a man, how to respect a man or how he should treat and respect me. Not to mention loving a man. How could I have given a man something I never had. It also caused me to look back on my life and recognize the generational curse.

I also became a young mother at the age seventeen. I found myself pregnant and single. At the age of nineteen married and pregnant. At the age twenty, two kids and getting a divorce from an abusive husband. By the time I made twenty-one I was on child number three and single. At age twenty-eight I married for the second time. My mindset had not changed or anything from my past relationships, and I was expecting different results. Even though that relationship lasted 13 years, I was still empty inside because again I didn't have Jesus as the head of my life. This separation I didn't see coming, so it was very painful. Not only did I love my husband, I was also still in love with him. It's a pain I wouldn't wish on my worst enemy.

Through all of it, it turned out for my good and God got the glory. It drew me closer to God. I turn and ask God to show me myself, so I can be a better person, mother, sister, friend, and wife. And he did. I didn't realize how lost I was, but I thank God for a renewed heart. I didn't realize the next thing I had to complete until, I was standing outside talking with my dad one day, and when I got ready to leave, I asked him for a hug. He didn't even know how to hug me. When I got in the car I just cried. My daughter asked me what's wrong? I replied, you know that's the first time I ever got a hug from my dad in 51 years. I just sat there and cried like a baby, because at this point, I realized my dad not being in my life did affect me.

Despite the lack of my natural father's capacity to love me, I thank my Heavenly Father for always being there. There is no greater love than God. This has been my continued prayer moving forward and I believe that if I remain in this posture before God, that He will continue to work in me, through me and for me.

This is my continual prayer. Father God, I Thank you for loving me when I didn't love myself. There is nothing or no one that will separate me from you. For you I'll live and for you I'll die. I tried it my way, and it didn't work. Now I'm doing it your way. Your way has given me peace, joy, and happiness, something no man was able to give me, and for that alone I thank you.

Signed the child that was always loved.

My Butterfly Story
Dr. Cynthia B. Brown

*And we know [with great confidence] that God [who is
deeply concerned about us] causes all things to work
together [as a plan] for good for those who love God, to
those who are called according to His plan and purpose.
(Amplified Bible) Romans 8:28*

My phone rang in the early morning hours on Thursday,
May 3, 2012. I was sleeping in, so I didn't answer. I had
taken the day off work to celebrate my 48th birthday. My
phone rang again. By the time I got up to respond, the ringing
had stopped. My husband had taken the day off work to
celebrate with me. Our youngest son, a senior in high school,
was exempt from the end-of-semester testing. The phone
rang a third time. It was my birthday, so I thought my family
and friends were calling to wish me a happy birthday. I
started to listen intently to messages. However, there was
one message that would change my life forever.

I picked up my phone to listen to the messages. As I heard
the news, sheer terror and grief were overtaking me. I woke
up my husband and youngest son, informing them we needed
to go to the hospital. Our oldest son was experiencing a
medical emergency. We drove in silence, each saying our
own prayers. My mind began to wonder that the worst-case
scenario would be that he may be in a coma.

We arrived at the hospital, went to the main desk, and
proceeded to the emergency room. I gave them our name and

the name of our oldest son. Eventually, we were led into a small conference room. After a short time, the door opened. The emergency room surgeon, priest, preacher, and counselor entered the room. I saw their lips moving, but could not comprehend what they said to me.

Our oldest son, Waymond II, passed away Thursday, May 3, 2012, my 48th birthday, from sudden cardiac arrest; he was 23 years old. I started to scream, cry, vomit, and collapse all at the same time. I just knew that I had to be with him at that moment. The staff brought a wheelchair and took me to the room where his body was. When I looked at my first-born son, my baby, Waymond, he had such a look of peace on his face. I could still feel his presence in the room. He was warm to my touch; I kissed him and told him how loved he was. At that moment, my life scripture Romans 8:28 I could not understand.

This feeling of loss, burying your child, was all too familiar. My middle son Wesley was born in October 1990. Our son lived for 23 minutes and then died from Potter's Syndrome. In my womb, Wesley was very active, responded to his daddy's voice, and had a strong heartbeat. So, how could this happen again?

Let's start at the beginning. My husband and I were married on May 9, 1987, we were blessed with three sons. Our first son was born in 1988, the second in1990, and the baby was born in 1994. We both grew up in church; however, on September 4, 1990, I was compelled to get baptized FOR REAL, and I was seven months pregnant with Wesley. Our oldest son accepted Christ when he was 11 years old. Our youngest son accepted Christ when he was nine years old. As a family, we were very active in church. My husband is an ordained minister. I am an evangelist. Our oldest son writes, sings, and glorifies God through Christian rap. The baby boy and I participated in some of his performances. Although we are not perfect, we pray as a family, teach the scriptures in our homes, and help the homeless.

Now maybe you can see why at that moment and for several years, I could not understand Romans 8:28. I did not comprehend how the death of my two sons was going to work out for my good and God's glory. The overwhelming, unbearable despair and grief consumed me for nine years.

The beginning of change started while I was sitting in a chair, grief-stricken. Our only living son, Kristopher, kneeled and, while holding my hand, asked why I had abandoned him. I looked at him intently, saying I had not abandoned him; I was here with him. He looked at me with tearful eyes and said, yes, you have; you have left me emotionally. It was then that I began to fight to come out of the pit of hopelessness.

During my wilderness experience, I tried to get rid of this pain with addictions to shopping, drinking to excess, smoking cigars and eventually cigarettes, overeating, and overworking. I needed true deliverance.

My village of family, friends, prayer warriors, mental health counselors, doctors, and therapists helped pull me out of this dark, familiar pit of hopelessness. I felt what seemed like heavy coats being removed from my body physically.

Zechariah 4:6 Not by might, nor by power, but by my spirit, saith the Lord of Hosts. (KJV)

This is where my butterfly story is birthed.

Before we continue, let's talk about the butterfly's life cycle. Romans 8:28 is my life scripture, and the butterfly is my life symbol. I believe that butterflies are beautiful, but they have not always been that way. However, before the birth of something so beautiful you must go through some painful and often ugly stages.

According to science, the butterfly has four critical growth stages: the egg, caterpillar, pupa, and finally the beautiful butterfly. Just like the egg, I was a babe in Christ when I was saved. I became a caterpillar; I could not get enough of the Word of God. My thirst for His truth was unquenchable! I prayed several times a day, attended every church service, went to revivals, hosted a ladies' ministry in my home, and completed online and correspondence biblical courses. I fed the spirit of God within me and consumed His truths and promises.

I believed that I would only live in the spirit world, and nothing could hurt me in the natural world. Oh, how wrong I was because we live in a fallen world. I was living, walking, and breathing Romans 8:28. It was then that I entered the butterfly pupa stage, a time of transition and considered the most dangerous. While in this stage the caterpillar outgrows its skin several times. It then enters a chrysalis silk cocoon while undergoing metamorphosis. The pupa totally depends on the chrysalis for protection from all outside elements. During this transition, the pupa is vulnerable as it hangs on a tree limb, barn door, lamp post, street sign, etc. While in this stage, the pupa is threatened by high winds, rain, hail, excessive cold or heat, animals, and other insects. But the pupa is protected by a chrysalis.

While I was in the pupa stage, my sons Waymond and Wesley died. I believed because I was trying to live according to the Word of God these things were not supposed to happen to me! The death of Wesley happened one month after I was baptized. And my first-born son died on my 48th birthday. Instead of being happy on my birthday, this was a yearly reminder that my son died. But in my pain, grief, despair, darkness, and sorrow God was doing something new in me. Now I know this could only be accomplished by going through the trials and tribulations that were tailor-made for me. God knew that I would need His word that I had consumed to sustain me. Although this was the hardest thing I have experienced, I was protected by the Word of God. Even when I thought and did not want to be protected. The Holy Spirit was with me in my pain.

However, when the stage of metamorphosis/metamorphoo was completed, God did a new thing within me. Metamorphoo is a Greek word defined in the New Testament as changing into another form, transforming, to transfigure. I was being changed from the inside out. As you read this, you may be saying to yourself, what does this have to do with a butterfly? During the pain of my metamorphoo, the Holy Spirit revealed my purpose.

I am called as an evangelist in the deliverance ministry. Instead of dying in the sands of grief, the WayWesX17 (WWX17) Homeless Project was born. A Texas-based non-profit organization with a passion for serving the homeless community. Just maybe while you are in your butterfly phases, God is trying to birth something new in you!

Isaiah 43:19 For I am about to do something new. See, I have already begun! Do you not see it? (NLT)

Evangelist, Dr. Cynthia B. Brown

Evangelist, Dr. Cynthia B. Brown, recently completed her PhD in Multidisciplinary Human Services from Capella University. Her dissertation focused on "Chronic Homelessness From A Paraprofessional Perspective". Additionally, Dr. Brown is a 2017 graduate from the University of Southern California with a Master in Social Work. She also holds a Bachelor of Science in Business and Public Administration, and a Post-Baccalaureate in Human Resources.

In 2015 Dr. Brown formed The WayWesX17 (WWX17) Homeless Project, a 501(c)3 Texas-based nonprofit organization. The origins of the organization are embedded in her being determined to overcome the grief of the death of her sons in a positive way. Waymond II died from sudden cardiac death at the age of 23. Wesley Pearce died from potter's syndrome after 23 minutes of life. Instead of dying in the sands of grief she started this organization. WWX17 mission is to use our collective voices to help restore hope, provide refuge, and create a legacy of global social change for all who are journeying through the grief of homelessness.

She has been married to her soulmate Waymond Brown Sr, for over 34 years. They have an adult son Kristopher and a wonderful daughter-in-love Priscila. Kristopher and Priscila, has blessed them with two beautiful granddaughters, Aria and Ainsley. Dr. Brown has five sisters and an awesome mom, Wilma Smith.

Faith Through the Fire
Janelle Rochelle

There are times when we will experience major losses in life, disappointment, and pain. However, bad times must be endured to make us appreciate all of the good times. I want to share my testimony of how after experiencing a house fire I doubted my faith- but in the end I learned the greatest lesson of God's love through what I thought were unanswered prayers.

It was a warm sunny day in November of 2014, just days before Thanksgiving, and I started my day as normal and was headed to work at 7:00 AM. As I warmed up my vehicle, I prayed to the Lord as I always have done for safety and protection as I traveled, for my children as they walked to school that morning, and I prayed that everything in my home will be as it was when I left that morning. I felt confident in knowing that the Lord heard my prayers as I drove to work without a care. What happened that afternoon was life changing as I received a telephone call letting me know that everything that I owned, and all of my possession went up in flames- let me explain.

I received a phone call from my children's school, alerting me that my home was on fire. At first, I did not know what to believe. And I thought that they may have the wrong telephone number. "Janelle, your house is on fire- you need to get here now!" said the voice on the other end. My first initial reaction was shock and I immediately thought that my children were harmed or in danger, so my first question was "Are my kids, okay?" Yes, your children are fine". The school Principal assured me that my 7-year-old son, and youngest daughter aged 9 had returned to the school, and my home is burning down and that I needed to get home. In a panic I immediately got off the call, rushed to my vehicle and made my way home. The long one-hour drive-which was my normal daily commute to work seemed like days. I drove home in a panic; crying, praying and with so many questions in my mind and the feeling that this was the first time in life of feeling helpless and hopeless, and not because of the situation, but because my faith was being tested like never before.

I thought about the scripture, Philippians 4:13, that says "I can do all things through him that strengthens me", but I must admit during that time, I felt my weakest and as if I was losing my mind. Sitting in traffic I was relieved knowing that my children were okay, but just shocked from it all. I had to hold on to the words of Philippians 4: 13 and trusting in the Lord because during that time I was lost, confused, upset, and my emotions took over me. I finally made it to my home saw smoke, fire trucks and everyone in my home, putting out the fire. I stood outside in disbelief and shock, watching everything that I had earned and worked hard for go up in flames. After a few hours of calming the flames and clearing the smoke, I entered what was left of my home just to be told "It may have just been electrical" I'm sorry", said one of the firefighters. I stood still emotional, numb, and in disbelief with so many unanswered questions. Thankful to God that we weren't home, and my children and I were safe, however I needed strength so that I can get through the following days.

I say this to you; gratitude, faith, and praise should not only be practiced when things are going right, but even during the hard times and tribulations. I must admit, I questioned God that day. "God- Why me? Lord, I prayed to you and asked that you protect my family, and you protect my belongings", were my thoughts during that time. Lord, I thank you for protecting my family because we are all safe and we're all standing here alive, but I can honestly admit during that time I was very confused that he took everything away from me- but this was the test! After praying I came to realize that I went through this because it was needed. Days went on and staying with family and friends became very stressful and I began to become depressed- I stayed in deep prayer. During my alone time with God one morning, He whispered to me, "You will put me first!"-that was when I realized the reasons of why I had to endure that bad experience; my priorities were out of order.

 Many times, we worship different things and not realize that we're doing so. We may idolize friends, our hobbies, the people that we spend the most time with, and not realize that we are not putting God first. When I heard God say that to me, "you have to put me first", I knew that this was a lesson for me, that I cannot go through life, wanting to gain materialistic things, achievements and accolades and not put God in it! I reached an epiphany during this terrible time and traumatic event and realized that my priorities needed to be reset. While I loved God and thought that I had a relationship with Him, as I think back on things now, being obedient and serving Him only was not a priority during that time.

So those things that took place in the event of my house burning down and leaving with the clothes on my back and nothing else devastated me. However, I had my health, my strength, my children, and my sanity. And that was the day that my faith was tested. God restored everything that we lost just weeks before Christmas. We regained everything that we lost a thousand times over. Blessings came from many people, but it was not the material things that I was thankful for. I was thankful for the lesson, and I was thankful for life and a renewed mind. I was going through a terrible time trauma, a tragedy, but God was with me, and he walked me through, and he taught me that He comes first! Your family, your loved ones, friends, your spouse, significant other, etc., are all part of your life and although they are important, life must include a solid foundation. Having Christ as the center and putting God first will strengthen your faith.

You may have experienced a loss rather its possessions, a family member, a friend, but I'm here to say even during times of loss, trust God and have faith! If you have a solid foundation and you put God first, he will restore everything that you've lost, and he will give you much greater in the end. Thank God for His promises and believing that His intentions for us are greater than our own.

Romans 5: 3-5 says, "Not only so, but we also glory in our sufferings, because we know that suffering produces perseverance; perseverance, character; and character, hope. And hope does not put us to shame, because God's love has been poured out into our hearts through the Holy Spirit, who has been given to us"

Proverbs 3:5-6 says, "Trust in the Lord with all thine heart; and lean not unto thine own understanding. In all thy ways acknowledge him, and he shall direct thy paths."

Janelle Rochelle

Better known by her pen name Janelle Rochelle, Janelle Rochelle Dye is a fervent author with a strong penchant to encourage, instill a sense of empowerment, courage, and strength in her readers by sharing her relatable experiences, trials, and triumph that many of them resonate with. In her rich authorship journey, Janelle puts millennials and women at the central focus of her works as she teaches them how to overcome obstacles, adversities, and feelings of giving up in life.

In an authoring journey debuted by writing poems at the tender age of 10, Janelle has authored several books. Her latest is *Mind Games 'N Dirty Talk; Daily Affirmations Can Empower & Encourage The Mind*, released in December 2021. Moreover, she is a co-author of *The Untethered Woman*, an international Best Seller in December 2019. Honored to be a part of this fascinating book compilation, Janelle will be focusing on how her faith has been tested and how she overcame the adversities. All her works are available on Amazon Kindle, and you can get a copy through her website authorjrochelle.com.

Currently, Janelle lives in Baltimore, Maryland. Whenever she is neither tucked in her tight work schedules nor writing, you will find her traveling, shopping, and spending time with her children. As an individual who doesn't buy the idea of being constrained by circumstances, Janelle has sought self-improvement all through and her latest achievement is graduating with a Master of Science degree in Management from Colorado Technical University in 2020.

Is This The End?
Dyraunique Williams

I can remember it as if it were yesterday, October 24, 2003. A Friday to be exact. I remember going to school, telling my sister I didn't feel well not thinking much of it. It wasn't until lunch time and while heading to the restroom I began to feel lightheaded. I passed out hitting the ground knees first. I was taken to the nurse's office, where my parents were contacted and told to take me to the emergency room. I remember my mother walking me into the emergency room and a male nurse immediately coming up saying he had a room for me.

Every time I reflect on this experience, I thank God for that nurse. I consider him an angel that God placed there on my behalf. After being admitted into the hospital, I remember the doctor coming into the room talking to my parents and telling them that if they had brought me in any later, I would have died. I had been bleeding for some days. I was a beginner when it came to my menstrual cycle, and I thought it was normal. At this point that was no longer the case for me. I was a 15-year-old girl that was hemorrhaging and passing blood clots so heavy you would have thought that I was passing a bowel movement. I know it sounds gross, but this is what it was I was going through.

What a woman having a miscarriage goes through is what the doctor said I was experiencing. I remember the doctor placing me on bed rest, saying that I would need a blood transfusion. They ended up transferring me to Tulane Hospital in the city of New Orleans. One of the scariest moments was while being admitted, the nurse was preparing to insert an IV and no blood came out when she inserted the needle. She ran out of the room. It was then that I knew something was seriously wrong. Little did I know that I would spend a week in the hospital. I received 12 blood transfusions, had a bone marrow done etc.

I remember my family coming in donating blood for me. I was so pale from the loss of blood that even the doctors on the floor were in shock because they had never seen anything like what was going on with me. My blood count was 3.6, I was considered the walking dead. At that time Tulane Hospital had the top hematology department and I had been blessed to have two of their top doctors working on me. They began to test me checking for what it could be. Every test they read came back negative. I remember them saying they couldn't find out what was wrong, so they began to test me for foreign diseases. I remember one specifically called Von Willebrand's. It was like every time I received a transfusion, the more blood I was losing.

At this point the goal became to stop the bleeding, and no one knew how long it was going to take. The doctors issued medicine that didn't help. I remember taking 10 pills a day. At this point everything had just become exhausting, and we had no date on when I would be going home. All the doctors knew is that I was bleeding and there was nothing that they could do to stop it. This is where I began to think, "Lord am I going to die?" I began to prepare my mind as if this was it for me. It was a very scary experience, but I didn't know what else to do. I couldn't stop bleeding and that is what I knew.

It was Thursday night October 30, which was my mother's birthday. I remember my uncle coming to the hospital to bring her a gift and some food. She stepped outside of the room while talking to them and to prevent me from seeing her cry, but I heard her. As I lay there in bed I began to talk to God, and I begin to say, "Lord I don't wanna die!" I'm only 15, I haven't even lived yet. Later that night while my mom and I were watching TV, I heard a voice say to me, tell her tomorrow we're going home. I immediately repeated to my mother what the voice had spoken to me. When I first said it to her, she kind of gave me that look like it must be those meds. Then the Voice spoke to me again saying to tell her God said we're going home tomorrow. When I said that to her, she replied, "If God said we're going home tomorrow, then we're going home tomorrow." I had no clue what had just taken place, but what I can say is I woke up the very next day October 31, 2003, spotless and that day I went home. What an experience to remember, it was my first time I heard the voice of the Lord. I wish I could say I knew that It was God at the time, but I didn't. Knowing that came with spiritual growth. What I did know at that very moment was I had just received a miracle!

I pray this encourages and touches the hearts of many facing sudden experiences. The word of God is true about childlike faith. God spoke and I believed without a second thought. I said what He said, and it manifested. I believed what the Lord spoke to me. May this increase your faith and cease all doubts and everything that is opposite of what our Father in heaven has spoken over your life.

Dyraunique Williams

Dyra W. is a humble servant of the Most High God. She was born in Gretna, Louisiana, and is an aspiring artist and Visionary of Serafina's Daughter LLC.

My Life Changed
Daphne Monchaud

I can remember growing up as a child living a normal life. My brother and I playing in the backyard, running, and jumping around doing flips. We had a big yard with a lot of space. My brother and I would see who could do the best flips. He would go first and do three flips in a row, very impressive. Now for my turn of course I had to be extra and run around the yard really fast and began to flip. I flipped so many times and fast you would have thought I took gymnastics. My brother was so amazed and shocked, he asked me "how did I do that," I really couldn't believe it myself. We laughed hysterically just having fun playing and enjoying each other. Those were the good ole days.

Then suddenly, our lives were changed drastically. I remember it so vividly. It was the coldest winter ever, November of 1988. My mom had gone out with a few friends and to our surprise would never return home. There was a knock on the door. It was a policeman. Anytime a policeman knocks on the door, it's never good. He came to report a single black female was hit Friday night and had been identified as Rita Monchaud. All I remember is my grandmother screaming "Oh Lord!" My brother and I started crying frantically just hearing this devastating news. I felt numb and confused not knowing how to process the news. I was ten, my brother was twelve and my little sister was only 2 months old. All we knew was that our mother who took care and loved us with all her heart, was gone.........

My mother was only twenty-eight years old. After her death my siblings and I were separated. We all went our separate ways living with one of my mother's sisters. My brother moved to New Orleans, I stayed in St. Rose and my little sister moved to Luling. After the separation I began to shut down, became depressed, and was very angry.

I remember at the age of thirteen contemplating suicide. I wasn't happy. I just lost my mother and now my siblings. I didn't feel loved. I remember I heard a voice so profoundly in my head and He said I love you. Not knowing what that was or whose voice I heard, it stopped me from taking my life. I didn't understand back then that it was the voice of God. We never grew up in church, and my mother's side of the family was Catholic, so when we did go it was like we were only there for 30 minutes then we left.

I never fully understood why we went to church because I never saw the evidence of change or Christ for that matter growing up. I remember going to school in the fourth grade, and I used to struggle with reading and understanding words. My fourth-grade teacher had given us an assignment to write a tall tale about Paul Bunyon. We had to read it in front of the class. I was nervous because I struggled at the time with pronouncing words. I always had a vivid imagination, so writing wasn't the problem, it was reading and spelling words. I was embarrassed of that because I didn't have anyone to take the time with me at home to help me become a better reader.

A few years later in the seventh grade, my older cousin introduced me to this author E. Lynn Harris. When I began to read his novels, I was intrigued by the large words and whatever word I didn't know I looked it up in the dictionary. This caused me to have a better understanding and my comprehension skills developed. I always spoke well, meaning proper. My aunt used to work for this prestigious law firm and always made sure we spoke correct English. I was always smart and inquisitive, always wanting to know something. I just knew I wanted to be a journalist or a schoolteacher when I grew up. I always was that child who asked a lot of questions and was always in someone's business, they called that nosey. I used to play with the neighbor's kids acting like I was the teacher, and they were the students.

Growing up I didn't have a brother and sister relationship with my siblings. Instead of having that brother and sister relationship we felt more like cousins because we didn't grow up together in the same house. My sister didn't find out we were her real siblings until she was thirteen years old. My aunt who raised her never told her that we were her biological siblings. She thought my cousins who she grew up with were her real brother and sister. Imagine how that made me and my brother feel.

My brother started rebelling, stealing my aunt and uncle's car who he lived with. He started smoking weed as a coping mechanism to deal with his pain. Meanwhile I was growing up looking for love in all the wrong places. (In the streets.) When I entered junior high school, I met this guy who all the girls liked. He was very popular. We became friends and talked on the phone for hours and hours getting to know each other. He made me feel special and I thought he loved me. I remember him always in and out of jail telling me lies.

I was very naïve and gullible then. That had a lot to do with insecurities, and pain I was dealing with considering everything I had experienced so far. Rejection, abandonment, molestation, and lack of love. I used to feel ugly and unwanted like I wasn't beautiful. Then I remember hearing that voice again. I love you; you are beautifully and wonderfully made. Not knowing and fully understanding at the time that was the voice of GOD.

As I got older and went through some difficult and tough times God was always there for me. When I was twenty-one,

I started going to church with my best friend and her boyfriend's mother at the time. When I went to this Baptist church, I felt this warm feeling inside that I never felt before. When the pastor spoke, it was as if he was speaking to me, and I began to cry. I felt his words resonating with my spirit. As I explained the feeling to Mrs. Dorothy, she told me that it was the Holy Spirit. I went a few more times to church and accepted the Lord as my Savior and me and my best friend were baptized at Beacon Light of New Orleans.

Through my journey in life, I began to learn about God and develop a personal relationship with Him, seeking Him and reading His word. The journey hasn't been easy. I haven't always listened to His voice, but He has always been there even when I didn't realize it. As I look back through my mess and even in times of disobedience, God has always had his hands on me never leaving me nor forsaken me. I give him all the honor and praise.

If you ever hear a voice telling you that you're loved, when you don't feel it, trust it. If you ever hear a voice saying life is worth living when you feel that it is, trust it. If you ever hear a voice saying you're worth it, you're amazing, you're strong, you're beautiful, you can make it; trust it. God is letting you know He is with you and He's keeping you until you learn of Him. When you learn of Him, you'll want more of Him. God has greater for all of us, and He is with us in the journey.

God Knows Best
Deborah Hunter

I didn't have a perfect life growing up, but I tried to live my life in a manner that was pleasing and right before God. I refused to be sexually active as a teenager, so I married at the tender age of sixteen and had my first child at the age of seventeen. We were young and not at all prepared for the roles we stepped into. We were unable to sustain ourselves, going through the ups and downs of adulthood, and ultimately the marriage ended in divorce before I turned twenty.

This left me with a daughter to raise on my own. I married again only to have that marriage end in divorce in a few short years. Once again, I was all alone, not knowing what I was doing wrong. I made a conscious decision that I would seek the help of the Lord in choosing my next husband because I desperately wanted to get it right.

I've learned what you ask God for, you just might get it. I humbly prayed to God and confessed that I messed up twice picking a mate, so this time I was going to trust Him to send me a husband of His choosing. He made me and He knows who He created for me.

God always answers our prayers, but not always the way we expect Him to. I thought my king was going to be tall, dark, handsome and without children. I described him that way to God. When I finished telling God what I wanted, I ended my prayer by saying, "Once again Lord, I messed up twice before so I'm going to shut up and trust you."

God blessed me to meet and marry the man who would change my life. Honestly, I questioned Him about the man before I got to know him. My first response was, "Lord, I know you are not sending me this short man". However, as time went by, I knew that he was the answer to my prayer.

My king was short, toast brown, handsome, and had kids. They were teens and older. He had the sweetest heart I have ever known. I learned this scripture Ephesians 5:22-23 "Wives, submit yourselves unto your own husbands, as unto the Lord. For the husband is the head of the wife, even as Christ is the head of the church: and He is the savior of the body;" and I had no problem submitting, because he treated me like a Queen.

Coach Melvin Burns was the best husband God could send me. When we picked our date to be married, he had a sense of humor with him. He told me to pick a month I wanted but don't use a month I had used before(smiling). He loved the Lord with all his heart and knew how to treat a wife. We both worked, but he got home first. He would have dinner prepared so many times when I got home from work. There was nothing he would not do. He helped with washing clothes and had our kids doing responsible chores to make life easy for us. My whole life changed because I trusted God.

The beginning of my teen life was rough, and I did not know how it was going to turn out. I stayed close to the Lord, and He worked all my mistakes out for my good. If I had my life to live all over again, I would make some changes, but I would still have my beautiful daughter, Tracy Sanders. She was the highlight of my life before my husband came along. We did everything together. I gave her my all and she gave me more than I could have asked God for. She was a very good student and by God's grace she attended college and eventually received her master's degree.

There was a little riff between Tracy and I when Coach came along because he cut into the time we spent together. As time went by, she got past the time she and I had together and really began to like and love him. They became close and were as tight as tight could get. Being a coach, he got her involved in sports, which wasn't her forte, but it kept her from hanging around the house in the summer's and becoming a wayward child.

God blessed us to adopt my niece, Dawn Price. Tracy and Dawn were very close and have the same birth date, ten years apart. They would celebrate their birthdays together like the sisters they were. We were a close-knit family and enjoyed the time we had together. When Tracy married her soul mate, Melvin proudly gave her away.

I was living what I call my best life for over fifteen years. I learned so much from my husband it is unbelievable. The areas I lacked, he taught me. We did everything we could together except travel. We were going to travel when He retired. He taught me to never put off tomorrow what you can do today.

New Year's Eve of 1994 our joy came to a screeching halt. Headed to New Year's Eve service in Algiers, LA we were rear ended in an accident. Somewhere between therapy and blood work for pain, Coach was diagnosed with cancer. He had what was called Multiple Myeloma. A disease of the marrow in his bones. We were told he had two to five years to live. After chemotherapy, he was in remission for a short time. When the cancer returned, it returned with a vengeance. We did not get the two years as we were told. He went to be with the Lord from our home on June 19, 1996. That day my life changed forever.

Fast forward ten years, God saw fit to bless me once again with my husband David Hunter. The ironic thing about David was one day I was having a pity party and crying on Melvin's knee. I said to him, "I'm here for you, but who's going to be here for me." He rubbed my head and told me "My poor little wife", that David was going to be my next husband." I looked at him like he was crazy. However, God confirmed it by telling me one morning as I was taking my shower. I prayed and told the Lord that I think I'm ready to marry again. He said to me, "Why are you asking me for what I have already given you? David is going to be your next husband."

Just like I didn't believe that Melvin was the one at first, I did not believe that David was the one, until I could not ignore God any longer. The Lord answered my prayer not once but twice. The rest is history, David and I married after Hurricane Katrina in June 2006. Through it all, the best lesson I've learned is, it's not a wife that finds a husband, but it's the husband God ordains that finds a wife. Let God do the choosing, and you'll find out God's knows best.

Faith and Stupidity
A.K. Jackson

Everyone has a "why." A reason that they react the way that they do, a reason they fight so hard, an experience or event that changed them, a reason they are faithful to something, whether it be good or bad. I love healthcare and helping people understand what goes on in their bodies and how to best manage it. I am passionate about educating others about their health. My "why" . . . is me! Many people know what I live with and what I love doing but not many know my experiences and how I got to the point where I am. This is my story . . .

Have you ever found yourself in a situation, but you didn't realize how deep you were in it until you were out? You didn't know how depressed you were until you were out. You didn't know how tired you were until you finally got some rest. You didn't know how overwhelmed you were until you got some help . . .or until you cracked. I've been in that type of situation too. For me, it was in the form of sickness. I knew I didn't feel like myself, but I didn't realize how bad it was until I cracked. My body gave up on me.

For months I had been getting sicker and sicker and not realizing that I was feeling bad and was that sick. Three weeks after my twelfth birthday, I became really sick at school to the point I was vomiting bile and almost passing out. My mom rushed me to the Emergency Room. While waiting to be seen, I slipped into a coma. It was then that I was diagnosed with Type 1 Juvenile Onset Diabetes. I was in this coma for four days while doctors worked to get my blood sugar down from over 3000 (normal blood sugar range is 90 – 110).

I was surrounded by praying people, friends, and family and I wish that I could say that their prayers and fussing kept me on the straight and narrow but that's not my story. My story is filled with over 17 years of ups and downs with my health. My story is filled with scores and scores of ER visits and hospital stays across Louisiana, Texas, Arizona, and Indiana. I wish that I could say that I took my health seriously and did what was necessary to stay on top of the diabetes, but that's not my truth. My teenage years and early 20s were filled with rebellion. The thing is, I was the only person that could feel the physical pain of that rebellion. I had faith that God could heal me of this horrific disease, I believed that with everything in me. At the same time, I didn't think that I deserved it. Literally EVERY single story I would hear about people's family members who had diabetes ended in their death from complications of diabetes. Their stories usually included amputation of their toes, foot, or leg. It included blindness, kidney failure, and years on dialysis. What made me so different from them that I would be healed when they weren't? The fear of that shook me to my core. I didn't want that, so part of me allowed my health to fail so that I could die young and quickly (I know . . . crazy, right?!)

Therefore, my chapter title is Faith vs. Stupidity. It was only stupidity that would make me believe that not taking care of myself would take me out more quickly with less complications, that doesn't even make sense. Fear will make you do some strange things, even when you know and believe differently. Fear will manifest itself as other things, including rebellion and stupidity!

Even in that stupidity or we can say lack of faith, God showed me that dying at a young age from diabetes was not in His will for me. One ER visit that turned into a hospital stay I remember so clearly that it clicked in my understanding of just how much God wasn't letting me go out like that. I was in the ER feeling pretty bad and the nurse was trying to start an IV on me. Out of nowhere she mumbled, "I don't know how you're even alive." I asked her what she was talking about and why she would say something like that. She said, "Your labs came back, and your blood sugar is 37700, you should be dead or at least in a coma!" This shook me and brought me to reality because people have died from blood sugars of 300 and 400 and here, I was walking, talking, understanding, and with my organs fully functioning. I was having blood sugars in the 300 – 500 range daily! I understood then that God MUST have something for me to do, some purpose for me. I had faith that He was keeping and had been keeping me all this time.

Okay God, if this is not your will for me, and you have so much purpose for me, why have you not healed me as I have had the faith that you would? (I know, I know, you're not supposed to question God. I needed answers and I did not have faith in anyone else to have those answers but God. Who else would you ask about a creation but The Creator?) It was then that God said to me, "Why should I heal you if all that you are going to do is continue to not take care of yourself and destroy your body?" That question hit me like a ton of bricks. I had faith that God would heal me, and I confessed that with my mouth, but I wasn't taking any action to take care of myself. According to James 2:26, I had dead faith! I was giving lip service and claiming my faith, but there was no action behind it. I wasn't doing the work required to take care of me. That was an insult to God.

The next thing is, what would healing look like? How could my healing be used to serve God? The natural mind would say that healing looks like not having diabetes anymore. While that sounds nice, that would be of no use and wasted 23 years that I have been living this life. My healing looks like living a fulfilled and whole life while still managing diabetes and doing everything that I shouldn't be able to do because this disease took years from me. My healing includes being able to help other people understand how to take care of themselves from the perspective of someone who is successfully walking in their shoes. My healing includes helping people who just don't understand how to manage with what doctors have diagnosed. My "why" to staying strong and committed to my health is me faithin it forward to help others who believe that diabetes is an automatic death sentence.

It is not God's desire for us to be sick and constantly fighting sickness in our bodies. 3 John 1:2, KJV says "Beloved, I wish above all things that thou mayest prosper and be in health, even as thy soul prospereth." How can we do His work in that condition? How can we enjoy His blessings in that condition? If God can keep me and my health, He can keep anyone. He has a divine purpose for your life, but you must believe and do your part! In that posture, FAITH wins EVERY TIME!

Be Transformed
Ischicka Jordan

"Do you not see what's going on?" My husband asked in a loud hysterical voice. As if I wasn't fully aware that the repo man was outside removing our vehicle from the front yard. I never moved, as I was so unbothered by the situation. It seemed as if I was oblivious to what was going on. As soon as my husband left the room, I was able to unmute the phone and continue hosting my business conference call without any rattled emotion. My husband at this point is really confused at the dynamics of our life.

A few short months ago I had a conversation with God to discontinue a business that I did not believe sat well with Him. I operated this business for over 15 years and had even experienced over 50k days, but I was tired of the money taking flight and going in circles because of some underlying practices that just were not right. I was riding home one day, and I said, "God if you can help me sustain, I will just find something else to do."

I was saying Lord I'm ready to walk upright, so now I need you to help us stay afloat with these heavy bills. I do not remember receiving an answer, but I can say that I started that night in a posture of leaning and depending on God.

With a husband you can imagine the decision to stop working wasn't easy. A few months prior my husband, who held a very well-paying job in loss prevention management for a billion-dollar company, encountered a huge lawsuit and had his entire department wiped out. The only thing that they offered him is severance to cover us for probably a few months and mental health counseling which he declined.

Yikes! What a fine time to make a deal with God regarding a career change. Some people may say that my decision was not wise, but I had confidence in the only wise God who is able to keep us from falling! Somehow, I had no fear, but you can understand why my husband was hysterical. It seemed like things were going downhill and he said that I was living in "la, la" land, which I was. It was a place of Peace that surpassed understanding. I was OK with people not understanding because I knew they would understand it better by and by.

Amid us figuring our next move out things started getting sticky. We were in a slump. Suddenly I kept hearing in my spirit to be transformed by the renewing of my mind. This made me feel that everything that I needed to run the shoddy company I could use to run a beautiful business. I have always been what I used to call a hustler, but that was the problem. I was always who God called me to be, but not fully being aware of who I was or what I possessed. I used my gifts the wrong way and was always from one hustle to the next. Nevertheless, I knew I had to get out of this slump.

I was then working with a network marketing company and every month we literally had just enough to the penny to get by. I knew in my knower that a transformation had to be done mentally to get me to where I needed to be. I begin meditating on scripture and watching motivational videos on YouTube just to pump my mind! Then the craziest thing happened. The words Quantum Leap registered in my spirit. I got up quickly, grabbed dry erase markers and literally wrote all over my mirror!

That moment, I decided to take control and transform my mind by what I put into it concerning me and God. I didn't just say it, I put it to action. I started writing things like "I am this" and "I am that." The declarations on that mirror were so big that if you looked at me then and cross referenced it with where I was, it would have seemed strange. It doesn't matter what I wrote, what matters is that I believed what I wrote and spoke. I wanted to face the words in that mirror every day until the person in the mirror lined up with the writing. As a plus, I knew that God and I had this thing going called seek first the kingdom of righteousness and everything else that I needed would be added.

Suddenly I had a burning urgency to get my real estate license. "Get your Real Estate License" I kept hearing. My response, ok I'll get my real estate license. I researched the information, took online classes, and understood everything. What should have taken a while I passed in 2 weeks. It was supernatural and was happening to and for me.

During this time of studying and acquiring my license I started hosting home buying seminars. My thoughts were "Ok God I'm still renting." His reply, "Teach people how to go from renting to owning." My response was "Ok." I would have sometimes over 100 people in the building to learn how they could go from renting to owning. I was so astonished by this success that I prematurely shared what I was experiencing with the wrong people, and they would mock me on Facebook saying things like, "Sis fix your credit first. Sis, get you a house first. How are you gonna show a house with no car?" These were actual Facebook posts about me because people knew that in the past, I had a 479-credit score, still renting and of course my car was repossessed. Before I could hang my license with a broker, I had a pipeline of clients that I did not have room enough to receive. I literally had to give some to other realtors.

As a result of referrals from that day to this one, I have never had a business card. It's like God put my name in the wind and blew it. Not even a full year of being a realtor I made more than 95% of realtors across the world. I even experienced everything that I wrote on that 6-foot mirror from top to bottom including experiencing a couple 6 figure months.

I put many people in houses before I bought my own and rejoiced each time because I knew that God has no respect of persons. I have since purchased 2 homes of my own and of course my husband and I both have transportation. I am thankful I moved when God spoke. I could have easily operated in fear, remained stuck and concerned about what people would think of me. Or even flaked on God and started back the hustle. I knew that if God was for me then No one could be against me.

I encourage you to renew your mind. Greater is in you, but your measure of great shall manifest upon your belief in God's greatness which is Big beyond our imagination. Close your eyes and imagine the greatest version of you. As soon as your eyes open you can literally be that person if only you believe. Tests will come to see if you really believe what you speak. Stand firm on your faith knowing you serve a God that is able to keep you from falling and can cause you to soar. My testimony is far deeper than I can express in this chapter, all I can say is "To be continued."

Faithful While Serving In Pain
Elder Juanita Johnson

When I gave my life to Christ, I wasn't perfect, but I took Him seriously. I had a hunger for the word of God and the more I read it and heard it, the more it became a reality in my heart. I began to apply these scriptures:

Romans 12:1-2
I beseech you therefore, brethren, by the mercies of God, that ye present your bodies a living sacrifice, holy, acceptable unto God, which is your reasonable service. And be not conformed to this world: but be ye transformed by the renewing of your mind, that ye may prove what is that good, and acceptable, and perfect, will of God.

1 Corinthians 6:19-20
What? know ye not that your body is the temple of the Holy Ghost which is in you, which ye have of God, and ye are not your own? For ye are bought with a price: therefore glorify God in your body, and in your spirit, which are God's.

Romans 6:14-16
For sin shall not have dominion over you: for ye are not under the law, but under grace. What then? shall we sin, because we are not under the law, but under grace? God forbid. Know ye not, that to whom ye yield yourselves servants to obey, his servants ye are to whom ye obey; whether of sin unto death, or of obedience unto righteousness?

Mark 12:29-31
And Jesus answered him, the first of all the commandments
is, Hear, O Israel; The Lord our God is one Lord: And thou
shalt love the Lord thy God with all thy heart, and with all
thy soul, and with all thy mind, and with all thy strength: this
is the first commandment. And the second is like, namely
this, thou shalt love thy neighbour as thyself. There is none
other commandment greater than these.

These scriptures helped transform and shape me into a
willing vessel to be used by God. As I continued in God, I
began to pray more consistently. Meanwhile, life's
challenges became more intense, and my body was going
through major changes. I was always a bit challenged in my
health from a child. There was always a weakness in my
body that I don't think my family really understood. My
family worked on a farm, and I believe to an extent, they
thought I was lazy and just didn't want to work. This caused
me to always push myself beyond what I could really handle
so they would not be disappointed.

As an adult, I would be in so much pain bringing the kids to
school, going to church, cooking, cleaning; committed to all
areas of my life. I was going through so many different
things, until the thoughts of worthlessness began to crowd
my mind, pain and sickness began to take hold of my body
and I began to walk in a bent state that resulted in surgery.

Through all of that, I had a pressing in my heart not to quit
pleasing God. I wasn't perfect but I knew God had a plan for
my life. When I accepted God as the Lord of my life, my
conviction was to faithfully serve Him no matter what was
happening in life. I learned in His word that I had to deny
myself, take up my cross and follow Him. I was determined
to live and to serve in His kingdom.

Aside from the physical challenges, I was unhappy in my marriage. I came up in strict holiness and getting pregnant out of wedlock was a no-no. The pregnancy of course meant we had to be married even though we were young. The marriage came with confusion, imbalance, frustration, disrespect, disappointment, and fear. It was my husband that caused me to know the Lord as my protector. I was in bed asleep one night, and the Lord allowed me to wake up and see my husband standing over me with an evil stare looking me in my eyes and said to me "I was thinking how I was going to kill you." I was terrified. We already had a horrible marriage and the thought of him trying to kill me was devastating.

He ended up leaving me for another woman and tried to take my son to live with them. One morning after bringing his girlfriend to work he was in a horrible car accident and passed away. In his passing there was sadness but even more so the peace. In all of this I still did my best to be kind, love others and serve God with my whole heart, holding fast to His word even though I felt broken.

There were still many life altering experiences. I had begun to wonder where God was in all this pain, and what had I done to deserve it. During my time of searching for help to get my life on a better path of peace, trusting people, of love, and financial stability, I looked to the church. A place where you should be able to trust, that would have my best interest at heart, that would love me to deliverance from the place of pain that you get from people of the world. Only to find out being vulnerable, caused me to be taken advantage of in the name of love and belittled and not accepted like others. I was single, not dating, loved God, trusted those who served God and was taken advantage of sexually by them. By now I feel like maybe I'm being punished for some reason or another, or maybe this is just my lot in life, so I would just make the best of it and take it one day at a time.

The disappointments seemed to be more than the encouragement. It seemed as if I was never going to have a bright future. Yes, I had a family who loved and cared about me, but I felt alone. Even in those moments, I continued to try to please God the best that I could in all that I had learned about living for Him. I knew a breakthrough had to come.

I remember right before the breakthrough, God gave me a song in my dream, "When I've gone the last mile of the way." The breakthrough came to pass. God sent a deliverer to rescue me and my family from the grips of deceivers. We were in a horrible pit. Just like the children of Israel in bondage, crying out to God, was my heart's posture. Just when it didn't seem like people were still used by the spirit of truth and the anointing of God, God sent me a Moses. No matter what we say or think in our walk with God in this life we still need deliverers that hear God, obey God and have been equipped by God to deliver.

I'll never forget, God used Prophet Patricia M. Frye as the deliverer of who came to the rescue. Glory be to the most high God! When we were set free, we became connected to her ministry and received the love and care of God for His children. Now it's a journey that is worth faithfully serving the Lord with joy and gladness from a place of Victory and wholeness. Now at 72 years of life, I can boldly say, I know too much about Him to doubt Him! He didn't bring me this far to leave me. Yes, weeping may endure for a night, but joy comes in the morning.

Elder Juanita Johnson

Elder Juanita W. Johnson is a humbled servant of the MOST HIGH GOD, the birth mother of two sons, Derrick (Angela) and Carlos (Cheryl)Johnson sr., the grandmother of four (3 girls and 1 boy) a sister to five siblings and an aunt who grew up with us as a sister. She was born in Hinds County Mississippi on 12-23-49, and raised in New Orleans, Louisiana, by her God-fearing parents the late Mr. Elihu and Mrs. Jimmie Lee Watts.

She has acquired Christian education, Biblical education and education through life's lessons. Her confession is her life has been and is being transformed by the renewing of my mind in Christ. Two of her favorite scriptures are Psalm 124, and Psalm 34:8. This journey in life has been filled with challenges only to find out that it's no longer I, but the Christ that lives in me. Galatians 2: 20b. I encourage you all to keep the faith and lay hold on eternal life in Christ Jesus.

My Truth and My Transition
Rose Greer

Sometimes, we get those really sour tastes in our mouths that leave us, even as believers and full of the Spirit, questioning the truth of God's love. If you've never been there, then you may never understand. As much as we all think we can relate with what Job went through, only a fraction of us really come close to that kind of pain.
The truth is I'm being tortured by my loss.
I don't look like me.
I don't feel like myself.
I can't find ME.
The changes in my life have changed me.
Somehow, I lost myself.
It's just hard to believe for better, when you've experienced nothing but worse over the last few years.
Loss made me believe God had forgotten me, all while I was sitting in church.

My capacity to question is rooted in His Intelligence.
My capacity to mourn and anguish is rooted in His Grace.
My capacity for despair and desperation is rooted in His Mercy.
My hope to heal is established in His Love.

I am not alone and He is NOT absent.
He is IN the pain
He is IN the sorrow.

I had no choice in all the matters that compromised me.

I have no power to rescue myself or my children from the loss of their older brother. I couldn't keep his heart beating. It wasn't my choice.

But right now, I have a choice. To accept God's will, with quietness and confidence. He never needs my approval or cooperation. Our lives are so transient, fragmented, and insignificant on the scales that He works. Our greatest delight, pleasure and security is to "watch Him in Wonder" Question as needed and Trust without wavering.

Peace, Peace, Peace

When people go through difficulties, it's not the outside noise that cause you to become depressed. It's a mental game of the enemy, a weapon of warfare formed against you from the start with the end goal of destroying you.

Pain, loss, COVID19, trials and tribulation are all channeled towards one goal destroying your mind. You don't die when you stop breathing, you die when you give up. This is what depression does.

When Satan wants to take something from a believer, he first attacks their peace. He attacks their confidence in God and gets them distracted. Never allow your pain to distract you. The moment your peace is jeopardized, you lose everything. If your peace is intact, you have really lost nothing, no matter what degree of devastation you go through.

As easy as it is to preach staying steadfast and unmovable during a crisis, it may not be so in reality. We get weary as humans. You must understand that there's an ongoing war. The devil is fighting hard to control your mind and you must fight harder to keep it. "Peace be Still"

"For the weapons of our warfare are not of the flesh but have divine power to destroy strongholds." 2 Corinthians 10:4 ESV

Did you get that? This is warfare! And guess what, you're a soldier, beloved. The devil may have come against you to steal, kill, and destroy, and that's okay. You must always remember there is One who is greater; He comes to give the fullness of life, that you may live. His name is Jesus!

The truth is, it is not unspiritual to be challenged but it is unscriptural to be defeated. Job, David, Ruth and Naomi overcame. So, when I look in the mirror at the shell of the woman that's left. I choose not to live in the story of yesterday, because it will define my today.

David, who I believe to be one of the most traumatized people in the Bible, declared in Psalm 34:18, *"The Lord is close to the brokenhearted and saves those who are crushed in spirit."* The term *brokenhearted* means "to be shattered into pieces." If you were to take a mirror and throw it on the floor, it would shatter. If you were to look at your face through that shattered mirror, you would see pieces of your face all over.

For many people, this is how they respond to trauma—they feel broken on the inside. Since they have been so wounded, they put up walls around their heart, walls of shame and guilt, feeling responsible for what has happened or what they have done. They shelter their broken heart because they don't want any more wounding. They may put on a mask of happiness and function in the world, but the reality is that they are so broken no one ever gets to see their real self because they are sheltered behind the walls they have put up.

Some translations of the Bible refer to the "crushed in spirit" as "contrite in heart or spirit," with the idea of contrite being "I'm sorry for my sin." The root word in Hebrew is "crushed." When you are crushed in this way, the weight of what you've seen or what you carry is so heavy that you feel crushed all the time. I hear testimonies from people who feel crushed by the weight of what they carry without knowing how to get rid of it.

David declares—and this is a wonderful promise—that God is near to the brokenhearted. He saves those crushed in spirit. In Psalm 147:3, David ups the ante and says that God heals the brokenhearted and binds up their wounds. There is a hope and promise that no matter how shattered you are or how much trauma you have been through, God is the God who heals the brokenhearted. He not only heals us; He binds up our hearts too. He brings shattered pieces of our broken heart back together so that we can feel whole again.

As I mentioned earlier, when someone experiences trauma, they can feel what I call "dis-integrated." This means that for them, it feels like the pieces of their mind and heart will never come together again. There is this piece over here and that piece over there, and the pieces never seem to connect. This is dis-integration. The only way reintegration happens to anyone is when Jesus Christ becomes the center of their life.

It says in Colossians 1 that the entire universe is held together through the power of Jesus. Not only did God create the entire universe; He literally sustains the universe, keeping everything together. The inference is that the planets are held in orbit, not by gravity, but the power of Jesus holding things in place. If that is true, then only by His power can we see a re-integration of our lives no matter how broken and chaotic they have become.

During the most disheartening, shattering, life-altering devastation of my life, the transition of my son seemingly transitioned me too. I FOUND HOPE IN what I had counted as a definite end to all I knew with the willingness to slip away in the self-imposed torment of God's abandonment. The hope was in knowing that I wasn't alone, abandoned, forgotten, rejected, or being punished. The same God that was in everything that exists is in my shattered pieces. My pain is real, but so is my purpose.

Rose Greer

An Arkansas native, A pioneering force in the ever-evolving staffing and insurance industry revolution. With over 30 years of insurance, and human resources experience. As a coach and trainer, she brings 'Common Sense thinking,' strategies, and implementation to her clients. Helping to align their people, processes, and procedures to impact their bottom-line profit. Rose Greer is a seasoned minister, trainer, coach, and consultant.

I Prayed For A Man and Not A Mate

Marie Delaney

In 1976 I was introduced to the man that would become my mate. He and I ran in the same circle but didn't see each other often. I was ok with being his friend because a mutual friend introduced us. At the time I was dating, but not looking for a life partner. The man I was currently dating wanted marriage but outside affairs as well. I was in college, working full time and wasn't sure of what I wanted out of life yet. I couldn't believe that this is the life God would have for me.

As long as I could remember I had always known God and had Faith. I am a dreamer and intercessor. By understanding the power of communication with God, my Faith grew, and my prayer life became stronger. I never realized God was trying to show me how powerful my prayers were. I was powerful in prayer, but my mindset was wrong, I was emotional and had no strategy in prayer.

I believed the word of God. The word of God says a man that finds a wife finds a good thing and obtains favor (Proverbs 18:22) I prayed to God and said this man said I was his wife but hasn't called yet. Now, at that time I related sex to love. The man I was dating wouldn't touch me but was having sex with other women saying he would marry me. All this while having another woman thinking he was going to marry her. I was 23 and hadn't had sex which caused me to feel like I wasn't in a serious relationship.
I will never forget going to a concert at the municipal auditorium and running into this man who said I would be

his wife with another woman. My heart was crushed. It didn't matter that I was with a man. I was not with the man that I lusted after, that said I would be his wife. I went home and lay on the floor and cried out to the Lord. I began to pray to God for this man by name. I began to fast and pray and ask God why this man who said he was my husband hadn't reached out. I didn't realize God was saving me.

I even prayed and asked God why this man I was with didn't show me he loved me. We had not had sex. This man was good to me. There wasn't anything material I wanted that wasn't too good for me. All I had to do was ask. I tried on several occasions tried to turn this man I was dating on, but he told me he was saving sex for our marriage. Saving sex until we get married never sunk in, especially since he was having sex with others.

I remember working with this elderly lady. She began to give me scriptures about sex before marriage. By this time, I had moved on from the guy I was dating. She gave me a good lesson about how sex didn't necessarily mean love and that the man saw what God had on me and valued it. I cried like there was no tomorrow.

I remember going to Marvin Gaye's last concert in New Orleans before his death. A group of us friends went together. To my surprise, the man I had been lusting over who had claimed me as his wife was there. I was surprised to see him because I wasn't told who would be attending with us. As they dropped me off, he told me you're going to be my wife. This time I wasn't laughing, my heart had been crushed.

My desire was to be loved, out of my parents' home and married. I thought if I had sex I was loved. I thought if I got married, I could leave my parents home. (My thinking was so wrong.) I pushed in prayer. I began to pray every day. Lord this man said he would be my husband. If I only knew at the time, I was looking at life backwards. I wasn't praying for a mate, I was praying for a man and calling his name out before God. I was praying intentionally, believing God would hear and answer.

God answered my prayer. I ended up with the man I prayed for who wasn't sure of what he wanted. The spirit of lust and my thinking of sex as love produced the experience. Right away this man I lusted after, seduced me. I had now sinned against my own body, the temple of God. I wanted out of my parents house by any means necessary, so I bit the bait I called to manifestation. I felt if this man got me pregnant, he would marry me and move me out. I see now how backwards I was in my thinking. I trusted God to get me out of my parents house but my way not His will. I was destroying my future, but God had a plan.

I remember a prophet telling me no matter what things looked like, I would have 2 sons. One would walk in their calling while the other would run. The word of God in 2 Chronicles 20:20 says, "Believe the Lord your God and you shall be established and believe the prophet and you shall prosper." I believed in God and even if I didn't know this man was a prophet at the time, something in me believed in the words he spoke over my life. I was praying for a man by name and calling forward what was spoken over my life concerning my sons. I was trying to rush prophecy.

My Spirit held on to that word even after I was told I wouldn't have children. I began to remind God in prayer what had been spoken over my life. I told God I believe him to be a man of God and God would not lie to me. However, I kept feeling like I needed to help the Lord. God showed me many times why he wasn't my mate, but I believed it was the enemy trying to keep me from my promise. I got the man I lusted for, and God had to develop him into the mate I desired. God was protecting me, and I didn't recognize I was warring against His protection. What I thought was the enemy because of what I desired, was really God covering me.

God promises to answer the just and faithful even if it's not His will, He will let you have it. How you handle what you asked for determines the outlook. You may get off course, leaning to your will but His purpose for your life must come forward. The word of God says a righteous man falls seven times but gets up again. Whatever you do, keep getting up. God is gracious, righteous, faithful, full of mercy and the God of a second chance.

My strategy in prayer has changed over the years. I have the wisdom of Solomon now. His word tells us, if we ask, He will answer us, and we shall receive. Allow the word of God to Shape your world and do the work. Get a prayer Strategy and work the word.
Signed,
 I Am Healthy! I am Wealthy! I Am Whole!

Mother Marie Delaney

Mother Marie Delaney is an intercessor who has been anointed by God to empower His people through prayer and teaching. She is a mother of two and New Orleans native. To connect with Mother Delaney please email mariedelaney@yahoo.com.

Shadows of My Past
Susanne McKeithan

Many times, in life people will underestimate, misunderstand, assume, and even judge your actions without taking the time to understand the reasons why you respond the ways in which you do. The events that happened in my childhood and adulthood were very tumultuous, heartbreaking, and abusive in every aspect.
My life has been filled with pressure, humiliation, treachery, and pain.

I can remember the day like it was yesterday. At the tender age of 3 years old, I started experiencing repeated molestation by my foster father. I can remember the confusing signals it would send to my young body. While I was not able to articulate what was happening at the time, I knew it didn't seem right. This was the first of many catastrophic encounters that began to shape my identity. I remember sitting on his lap, and him fondling my genitalia. I was an innocent defenseless 3-year-old girl, and I had no understanding or ability to protect myself.

At that age, your mind has no way of comprehending that you are being sexually violated. These early childhood violations later turned into patterns of promiscuity. I started associating sexual acts and desires with love. I was deceived into thinking that a man that desired me sexually must love me. Where I should have been covered, protected, shielded, and loved, I was compromised and violated. These violations created feelings of inadequacy and insecurities that shaped many of my future relationships with men. These very shadows that covered me captured me into shame and silence.

After I left my foster parent's home, I was adopted by my first family. This family played a major part in the downward spiral of events that added to the abuse I suffered prior. It increased my feelings of low self-worth and esteem.

As a result of being placed with that family, I became a victim of both verbal and physical abuse. I remember sitting at the table and being told how to pray over my food. After many attempts at saying my grace, my adoptive mother was not pleased with the way that I was speaking and threatened to beat me with the dog's chains. I was only 3 years old at the time. I had no idea that this type of behavior would continue for many years and food would be used as punishment for the smallest of things.

There were times when I was not allowed to eat or drink for several days at a time. I could not comprehend what I had done to deserve such horrible treatment. Oftentimes, I would be locked into my room and told not to come out. My adoptive mother would pour baby powder on the floor to make sure that I did not come out of my room. One day, I was so hungry I decided to try to jump over the baby powder to sneak and get some food. I jumped over it with joy only to find my adoptive mother on the other side pointing a gun to my face. I can still remember those scary words that she spoke. She threatened to "blow my brains out execution style" if I ever tried to get anything out of the refrigerator.

I was treated as a slave, forced to work in and out of the home and was not allowed to complete my schoolwork. At the age of 13, I could remember dreaming about how it would feel to be loved, accepted, and appreciated. Shortly after that, I started desiring to become pregnant. I wanted so badly to have someone that I could love and take care of. I did not know my birth parents, but I wanted an opportunity to right the wrongs I had endured by having my own child.

After a severe beating with an extension cord, I was removed from the adoptive family at 15 years old and placed back into foster care. While in foster care, I continued to be abused. In that home, the foster father would come into my bedroom while I was asleep and place his fingers in my vagina. This happened on several occasions and on one occasion he masturbated in front of me. Not long after that, I was raped by his brother. My virginity was stolen from me. I ended up getting sent back to my adoptive home where I stayed for another year before joining Job Corp at 16 years old. When I turned 17 years old, I found out that I was pregnant and was forced to leave Job Corp. As a result, I experienced bouts of homelessness.

By the time I turned 21 years old, I had been raped, beaten, and left for dead. I remember crying out to God and saying that there had to be more to my life than this I knew that God existed, and I decided to pick up the yellow pages and find a church to go to. That same day I had spoken with the pastor of the church. Later that week, I went to the service high on marijuana in total desperation. During the altar call, I felt like all eyes were on me. Nevertheless, I pressed my way to the altar and a lady met me there. I can remember her gentleness and love radiating from her touch. As she prayed with me, I remember feeling a strong power like I had never experienced. I wept and cried and gave myself over to the overwhelming feeling of love that I felt. I was baptized with the holy ghost fire at that moment.
From this powerful experience, I began attending church and developing my relationship with Jesus Christ. From that point on, I was never the same. I was finally at a place where I had the liberty and permission without restraint. This,

experience allowed me to be captivated by his presence, and I learned what real love looked and felt like. After submitting my life to Christ, I realized that God took every scar and created a picture of beauty. In my walk with God, I have found Him to be faithful to handle my secrets with care. God's love will embrace you in that moment. In Isaiah 61:3, the scripture states "To appoint unto those who mourn in Zion to give unto them beauty for ashes, the oil of joy for mourning, the garment of praise for the spirit of heaviness; that they might be called trees of righteousness, the planting of the Lord, that he might be glorified".

I pray His love will capture, rescue, and deliver you to his throne of grace. May you be filled with his glorious light, everlasting love, and grace.

"Daily Confession of Faith"

In Christ I am anointed and a powerful person of God.
I am a joint-heir with Jesus and more than a conqueror.
I am a doer of the Word of God and a channel for His blessings. If God be for me, who can be against me?

I am blessed coming in and I am blessed Going out. My enemies are fleeing before me. God has commanded His blessing on my storehouses. He has opened His Good treasures and I shall lend and not borrow. I am the head and not the tail. He has given me power to make wealth.

I dwell in the secret place I have His protection and provision. God is my refuge, my fortress; I am not afraid of the snare of the fowler. No Evil shall befall me, and no plague shall come nigh My dwelling. God has given his angels Charge over me and they are bearing me up in their hands lest I dash my foot against a stone, as declared in Psalms 91.

I Peter 2:9 establishes I am a chosen generation, A royal priesthood, a holy nation. I am a peculiar person called out of darkness Into His marvelous light.

I Peter 2:24 states, I have been healed by the stripes of Jesus. Cancer, sugar diabetes, heart disease, sickness, Afflictions, infections, or any other disease cannot enter my body. I am without spot or blemish, an intercessor, the righteousness of God, saved, and washed in the Blood of Jesus.

"No weapon formed against me shall prosper, and every tongue Which rises against me in judgment You shall condemn. This is the heritage of the servants of the LORD, and their Righteousness is from Me," Says the LORD. I am saved from wrath by Him and justified by the Blood of the Lamb.

Lord I pray that those may prosper that love Jerusalem and that peace will be within them and prosperity in their houses according to Psalms 122:6-9.

Hallelujah, Hallelujah, Hallelujah!

(Compliments of Christianword.org Red Prayer Book)